WITHDRAWN

W9-ABM-518

By Cross and Anchor
The Story of Frederic Baraga
on Lake Superior

By

JAMES K. JAMISON

Illustrations by Eleanor Dart

1946
ST. ANTHONY GUILD PRESS
PATERSON, NEW JERSEY

Copyright, 1946, by
James K. Jamison

Printed in the United States of America

BY
CROSS
AND
ANCHOR

He showed them a crucifix and told them its meaning.

(Page 89)

g. S. M. Frances Chantal

921
B231J

To

My Young Daughter

JANE

And to All Thoughtful Youth Everywhere

Who May Learn Herein the Power of Humility

FOREWORD

WHEN I was a child a Chippewa Indian boy gave me a pair of snowshoes and taught me to travel on them "like Père Baraga." Young Red Bird, the Chippewa, knew Father Baraga through the stories of his elders two generations removed. They were miraculous tales as passed on to me: a whole body of the folklore of a poor and isolated people inhabiting the environs of Lake Superior.

I have never forgotten those tales. There was something in them that impressed me so deeply that my interest in Frederic Baraga continued and expanded throughout my life. Those first impressions have now been sorted, catalogued, amended, corrected, amplified and, above all, contemplated.

So I am impelled now to tell the story. I use the word "story" advisedly: this is not an attempt to write either biography or history. But still less is it fiction. Of course, the conversations are not actually quoted from a historical chronicle; and for convenience, some characters (not many) have been invented. Yet people precisely like these were in contact with Father Baraga in the relationships indicated, and all of the conversations are true as far as purport is concerned. Every date, moreover, is historically accurate; every deed attributed to Father Baraga is founded on the record; every experience incorporated in the story is drawn from indisputable sources.

These sources are the words of the man himself, as he set them down meticulously in a journal — forthright words without quibble or extenuation — and as he described his work in America to those in Europe who sometimes contributed funds

[VII]

in aid of his missions. Thus he reveals his innermost light, often baring his soul in the travail of failure for which he blames himself; and if we impute to him thoughts in given scenes and crises we do so with such license as he grants us in his journal and his letters. But these sources are supplemented and illumined by the accounts of men, priests and laymen, who knew him and worked with him: descriptions of his appearance, his manner, his indefatigable zeal, his physical courage, and above all of the character of his spirituality, that rises to the stature of saintliness. These sources and acknowledgment of their several uses are listed at the end of the book.

Yet there is reason for presenting this material in story form. A story is the record of a struggle, whereas the biographer and the historian are not permitted the latitude necessary to focus attention sharply upon this aspect of life. The narrative of Frederic Baraga's mission is essentially the narrative of a struggle — long, intense, unrelenting — out of which a man emerges to victory.

Finally, in fairness to the subject, to the reader and to the author, I believe it needs to be said that this writer is not a communicant of the Church which Frederic Baraga served.

JAMES K. JAMISON

CONTENTS

CONTENTS

LIST OF ILLUSTRATIONS

[XI]

BY
CROSS
AND
ANCHOR

PRELUDE

THE old priest was very comfortable in a deep chair. He was only mildly aware of the restless pacing of the young priest up and down the room before him. He was not really paying close attention to anything. He was thinking a little, but not very much, about himself. What he thought was that here was a chair which must have been designed and built by a craftsman who realized there were not many chairs that would hold fat people safely. He could let his whole weight rest on this one — he didn't have to try to sit lightly and take little, short breaths not very deep into his stomach.

But then — so he was thinking and scarcely heeding his young colleague — all of the furniture in Castle Treffen was like that. He had seen it often and each time he had stopped to think about it a little. It was very fine to rest here; and perhaps the good Amalia would enter the room soon, and when she noted his presence would order some refreshments to be brought. Meanwhile he would discipline himself and give Father Frederic some attention. Presently. But he had walked a considerable distance striving to keep up with the too-swift pace of his young companion, and it was another of those hot, dry summers in the Suha Krajina, when the farmers were hauling water from the river because their cisterns were empty. Yes, age and weariness had overtaken him. More and more these days he realized that he had spent almost all of himself that he had to spend in the service of his parish. Now at last the time to rest had come, the time to sink back into old age and let energetic youngsters like this Father Frederic take over.

[1]

He roused, catching himself just short of going to sleep. That would have been unforgivable because he invited me here, he wants to talk to me, he is now telling me something that leads up to the announcement of some decision or other that he has made. Probably some small parish nuisance of no importance. . . .

As a prelude to the effort of giving his mind to what Father Frederic was saying, he fixed his attention drowsily on Father Frederic himself. If his voice were only shrill and loud, but no! He talks so low and his tones are so gentle that I am soothed when I need to be startled and waked up. And though he is a man, he isn't any larger than a good-sized boy — he could walk under my extended arm. And he wouldn't weigh half what I do — no, not half. About half my age, shall we say? Yes. I am sixty-three — he is half my age. Very well, my fine young man with your long brown hair and clear blue eyes — you have a very handsome look about you and you would certainly be quite a fellow, yes indeed, quite a fellow, if you were taller and heavier and —

". . . not my decision but the will of God! It is settled, Father Zajec!"

The somnolent old priest came to sudden full consciousness. The young man stood directly in front of him, not two feet away.

Father Zajec hadn't the slightest idea what was settled, but the time had come when he must say something. "Yes, yes," he offered. "Yes, I suppose so."

At that moment Amalia came into the room and he was saved from the immediate consequences of age and obesity and fatigue. He rose and greeted his hostess with great cordiality.

"It is not my decision but the will of God."

[3]

"My good Amalia!" he exclaimed. "Here we have been talking so absorbingly — your brother and I. He presents his points so convincingly — why, I scarcely realized you were with us!"

Amalia greeted Father Zajec with a warm, friendly smile.

"Yes, Father," she said, "I am afraid my dear brother is too convincing in this case. But now that you know of his decision, do you agree?"

"Oh, I see," the old priest temporized. "I take it, then, he has already announced his decision to you — is that the fact?"

"Yes, several days ago," Amalia told him. "But I asked of him one final favor — that he take counsel with you. You have known us as you knew our father and mother before us. And Suha Krajina has been the home of your people for many generations, as it has been of ours. One does not leave his native valley so easily. But I make no remonstrances, Father! Frederic explains that his decision is the will of God. If it is the will of God, I am resigned. It is on that particular that he promised to consult you."

"Very well, then," Father Zajec said. "Let us be seated." He eased himself back into his comfortable chair, but he was very much awake now, and considerably embarrassed. He looked at Amalia. She was older than her brother, an admirable woman, almost like a mother to the young priest. They were a rare family, these Baragas, he thought, recalling the solid goodness of their father Nepomuc Baraga, who had been so true a friend, and of the devout Katharina Jencic, their mother.

"And you oppose this decision, my Amalia," he began, clearing his throat, "only if it proves after all not to be the will of God?"

"Yes — but there are other matters to consider," Amalia

replied. "It is true that I have always lived here at the castle and managed the estate while Frederic has been away in pursuit of his studies. That has been quite a number of years — first at Laibach, then at the University of Vienna, and again at Laibach, in the seminary."

"Yes, indeed, Father Frederic has received a very fine education," the old priest assented heartily. Here at least was a point he was clear about. "Beyond the average for a parish priest — far beyond the average, I must say. A university graduate in civil law — think of that now! And the foreign languages! Besides his own Slovenian, to be able to speak equally well French, German and English — to say nothing, of course, about Latin! But we interrupted you, my good Amalia. Will you please proceed?"

"As you know," resumed Amalia, "our mother died when Frederic was eleven, and he was only fourteen when our father went. The estate was left to Frederic, as the only son. What you may not know is that he has conveyed his entire inheritance to me."

"But what of Antonia?" Father Zajec exclaimed, turning to the young man. "Frederic, is it possible you have given all to one sister and nothing to the other?"

"That is true, Father," Frederic told him. "Antonia is prosperously married. Sir Felix de Hoeffern will take good care of our little sister. And if anything unforeseen should happen in that regard, she can always return here to Amalia. So Antonia is doubly protected, you see."

"Well, well — indeed!" The old priest folded his hands over his stomach and contemplated the situation. "That would be a considerable property, my friends — a considerable property. It is years ago, of course, but I recall that your mother

[5]

brought a very handsome estate to your father. Part of it was Castle Malavas, where you yourselves were born. When your parents were still alive, I celebrated Mass in the lovely little chapel there. I should imagine there would be ample to provide very well for your sisters — very well, indeed!"

He spoke with friendly interest, though he disliked being consulted on such family questions. He did not want to meddle in people's affairs. If this young zealot had seen fit to make his priestly career a penniless one — well, there was no harm in that. He might be the better priest for it. And now Father Zajec would have to find a way to say all this to Amalia without seeming to give counsel either way.

But Amalia was speaking. "Not even an annuity, Father! When I could not dissuade him from settling everything on me, I urged him to arrange an annuity of a few hundred florins for himself. But, no, Father! Not even that, not even a hundred — not even *one florin* will he have!"

Frederic Baraga said with a quiet intensity, looking at neither of them: " 'The Lord is the portion of my inheritance and of my cup; it is Thou that wilt restore my inheritance to me.' "

The old priest scrutinized him and thought: Yes, he is a zealot. Ordinary human beings, even good ones, don't feel so deeply as this. And it is the more remarkable because he is so restrained. Why do you suppose he did not enter one of the Orders and become a monk? I will ask him. It will postpone the moment when Amalia will demand that I deliver wise and practical counsel, which, God forgive me, I do not want to attempt.

So Father Zajec said, "Tell me, my noble young friend, have you ever contemplated adopting the monastic life?"

Father Baraga looked at him in surprise.

"No, no, that is for others — it would not do for me! I could not pass a lifetime searching my soul as some men do. Whatever of sanctity God may bestow upon me must come through action and be used in action. I must go where men need to know Him. My soul must be fed the sustenance of service to others. I cannot avoid it. I cannot delay. There is an urgency here in my breast. It tells me to hasten, to be on my way. Therefore, I go at once!"

The strength of feeling behind his words showed in every line of his face. His eyes brimmed with tears. "I go at once" had the sound of utter finality, complete and irrevocable. It came upon the old priest like the voice of an ancient judgment.

"God bless us, Frederic, where do you go? What are you talking about?" he cried.

"America," Father Baraga answered, "as I told you."

The old priest looked at him as though he had never seen him before. So this was it!

Every nerve of Father Zajec's body tingled with awareness now. His reaction was immediate and violent opposition.

"Frederic Baraga of Treffen, I forbid it!" he shouted, hoisting himself to his feet. "Of course, I can't forbid it," he cried in exasperation, "but I would if I could, mark you that!" He paced up and down, stopping once near Amalia and exclaiming, "What are you thinking of, Amalia, to agree to such a plan?" After a time, when neither of the others had spoken, he returned to his chair. His face was very red but he was recapturing his mental processes.

He should not have been so vehement, he knew. But the sense of loss had overwhelmed him — personal loss, loss to his parish, loss of a support in his failing years. And there were other considerations: the young priest's safety and welfare, the proper use of his manifest great talent.

"Now, then," he announced, facing Father Frederic, "do you realize that you are a very frail young man physically? In stature you are below the average. In weight of flesh and bone you are about half of one of our good farmers here. You have never worked at manual labor. How long do you think you would survive in that rough, wild America? God bless you, you would die there in a year!"

"I am stronger than you suppose, Father," replied Frederic steadily. "When I was a student at the university, I spent my holidays and vacations on walking trips. I have walked from Vienna through Moravia, Bohemia and Bavaria, carrying a knapsack and preparing my own meals in the open. It is true that I am of slight stature but I have always been in good health, and perhaps I have a kind of wiry toughness. I shall be all right in America, I assure you. Even if I prove to be weak — why, God protects the weak."

"And punishes the foolish!" the old priest grumbled. "Well, suppose you could survive. Is it necessary to go half around the world to serve God? Here is your place! Your people have been here for centuries; you are sprung from roots deep in this soil, and here you should remain. Here, right here, are your obligations and your duties. Does not our poor country need its priests? And this parish — do you not see that it needs you?"

"But you are here, Father. And are there not other priests in our country?" Father Frederic asked mildly. "This valley of ours was served by priests as early as the fourteenth century; the monastery at Sittich was founded in 1135. Where I go there are no priests."

[8]

"But that is exactly what I am getting around to," Father Zajec rejoined heatedly. "You do not fit into that America. You have no background there. Here you are a Slovene. You are comparatively rich; you are of gentle birth. All that is wasted in America; while here — now that the Austrian Empire is becoming strong and powerful, favors will be given to men like you in these provinces. Why, years ago when Napoleon set us up as the Kingdom of Illyria (you were a mere boy in school then), the young men of that time who were intelligent and well disposed to the French made rapid progress in property and power. It is true, all that is gone now, and we are a province of the Austrian Empire, but even so, there are many ambitions to be realized right here in our own poor little Carniola. With your education and your knowledge of foreign languages, there is a place at court for you. You must think of your sisters and your departed parents. Don't you want to bring honor to the family name? I have friends, highly placed friends, whom I can approach and who will be glad — "

"Father, dear Father Zajec, God forgive me if I offend you! I appreciate with all my heart your sincere interest in me and in my family. But it is precisely here that I do not fit. You have outlined the scheme of advancement by fawning and intrigue that is the custom in kingdoms and empires. That is impossible for me. Oh, I do not condemn it. I can understand that another man might practice it in order to bring better things to many poor and worthy people. Across the sea, in America, there are no kings or emperors. Men there are all equal.

"But I do not want to be misunderstood. I do not go merely because that is true. I do not go for any political reason. Indeed, I know that even people who believe in political equality among themselves may become ruthless in their disregard for the rights of weaker and lesser peoples. That is happening in America. The tremendous energies of that great democratic people are forcing them across a continent. The original inhabitants, the Indians, are not absorbed by them. They are being driven ahead, in a long, thin, ragged line of retreat before this terrifying avalanche of mass thoughtlessness. Somewhere on that retreating line I shall find a place to perform my mission as a simple servant of God. If you ask me why, I cannot tell you except that I must. God wills it. With His aid, I shall give to the poorest human wretch on earth, hopeless and hungry and sore though he be, something that neither king nor commoner shall ever take away from him!"

The old priest was silent. Of course he knew Father Frederic's compulsion. And who can deny grace? The threat of loss and hardship that had roused his angry protest at first, dwindled to a very little barrier now, just as it must have done before Father Baraga's own intention, he knew. He raised his head to see Amalia looking at him meaningfully. Frederic Baraga was as remote from both as though an ocean already intervened between them.

At this moment a young woman came into the room, followed by a stalwart and comely young man. Quickly sensing the tension, they stopped hesitantly as though to withdraw.

But Amalia said, "You are back from your ride already, my dears! Do come in and sit with us. Antonia, please tell Maria to bring cakes and milk."

Father Zajec returned to abrupt consciousness of his surroundings.

"Ah, milk and cakes! The milk rich and cool, and the cakes spiced with caraway seeds! Yes indeed, the refreshment is welcome. And, Frederic, you too must have some." The old priest's voice had a note of placative appeal.

Maria entered bearing a large stone mug filled with milk and a plate of small cakes, which she set on a taboret beside Father Zajec's chair. Soon he and Sir Felix were eating and drinking, Antonia had seated herself on an ottoman beside Amalia, and the room assumed a pleasant air of sociability.

"I hope I'm not intruding," said Sir Felix to Amalia. "If you are discussing some family matter, I shall be glad to return for Antonia a little later."

"No, no," Amalia told him. "We were talking about Frederic's going to America, of course. There is nothing private about it. Besides, you are one of the family now. Please make yourself comfortable."

Antonia, a frail figure of a girl without any of Amalia's robustness, exclaimed, "Isn't it wonderful, Father Zajec — Frederic's going to America! I think it's so venturesome and romantic."

"Well," the old priest said, scowling at the cake he held before him, "whatever else may be said about his going, I do not believe we can accuse him of going on a romantic adventure. I know him too well for that! Now, if it were Sir Felix — "

Father Baraga rose, smiling.

"Father," he said, "will you excuse me for a little while? I am going across the field to see old Anton, who is sick. He has asked for me and I have promised to come this afternoon. I shall be back presently."

When he was gone, the old man turned to Sir Felix.

"Sir Felix, your wife was speaking of romantic adventures. Perhaps *she* would like a voyage to America?"

"O Father," Antonia cried, "you must stop teasing my Felix!

[11]

He doesn't know you as well as we do and he thinks you mean everything you say. I have to reassure him. I tell him I cannot remember from my smallest childhood when Father Zajec did not tease us children."

"No, Antonia!" Father Zajec set down his empty milk mug. "No, it has amused me now and then to tease you and Amalia, but I cannot recall that I ever teased Frederic. He has a most amiable good humor, but he is never frivolous."

"Oh, I know I am often frivolous," Antonia laughed.

"Well now, do not interrupt me," Father Zajec went on. "I will tell you an incident. I remember once when Frederic was a small boy, I came into the courtyard and found him nursing some blisters on his bare feet — stone-bruises or the like. I said to him, 'Well, young fellow, it's a great misfortune to be the son of a father who is so poor he cannot buy his boy shoes.' 'Yes, it is very unfortunate, Father,' he told me in a sad voice. His expression was so woebegone that I was forced to laugh. 'But why do you laugh at misfortune, Father?' His eyes were actually filled with tears. I said to him, 'I laugh at a boy who lives in a castle but has blisters on his feet because he has no shoes. Is that not amusing?' 'Oh yes, Father,' he smiled through his tears, 'I think *that* is very amusing!'"

"But something told me I had not been quite successful in teasing him. I came in and sat with your father, right here in this room. I said, 'Nepomuc Baraga, your boy is in the court-yard with blisters on his feet because he has no shoes. He and I think it very amusing.' '*I* do not think it is amusing,' Nepomuc said. 'Do you know what that young rascal has been doing, Father? He has been giving his shoes away to peasant boys as fast as I could buy them. Now let him suffer his blisters!'

"I remember telling him: 'Nepomuc, I think you are the

father of a son who enjoys blisters on his own feet if he can prevent them on the feet of another. That is extremely rare in this world. And I say to you further, Nepomuc Baraga, that you are the father of a son who will turn out to be either a fool or a saint!' "

Old Father Zajec was glaring at all of them. Suddenly he erupted from his chair and roared, "Who am I to give counsel? Who am I to try to turn him from his course?"

As suddenly, the strength seemed to be gone from him; his knees sagged and his arms hung limp.

"I have no wisdom," he uttered feebly. "I am a spent old man looking for comfort." His hand trembled as he reached out to help himself back into his chair. He sank down between the wide arms and sighed. "I have seen at last the power of humility," he said, and his voice broke in a sob.

"Dear Father," Amalia cried, "I have brought you all this trouble. You have exposed yourself to the hot sun, and your great anxiety for our happiness has caused you to overdo. Please forgive me! Sir Felix will help you upstairs and you can lie down in one of the cool bedrooms."

Father Zajec waved them all away.

"No, allow me to sit here quietly, my good Amalia. I shall enjoy listening while you others talk of your common affairs. That will restore me — to hear of the many little things that we think are important here in our Suha Krajina. Our little Antonia will chatter about the homely and comfortable things she has seen on her ride, and Sir Felix will tell us whose grape arbors look promising and whose cattle are thriving. Then, when the sun begins to sink and the cool of the evening approaches, Frederic will walk down the road with me, and I shall bid him farewell."

[13]

CHAPTER I

NO SCENE in all the world, he thought, could match it. He had entered upon it and been embraced by it before, but on this July morning in 1835 he thrilled with a new awareness. The atmosphere had a clear, sharp vitality. The expansive waters were incomparably blue and the crests of the small waves flashed under the high sun. Sails of numerous small craft etched the horizon and it seemed to him, even though he knew that they were on errands of commerce, that these must be cruises of pleasure. Over all the waters and upon the shores lay a profound serenity.

Mackinac Island, that sentinel of the straits connecting Lake Huron and Lake Michigan, lay ahead, small and fixed on the line of sky and water. Over upon his right hand the low shore of the land mass that is the great peninsula of Michigan was a long brown line that his canoe had been following for hours. Across the broad straits he could see the rugged highland of the northern peninsula.

In the straits the water was choppy with short waves kicked up by wind and current. The two Indians plied their paddles with increased diligence and caution. The canoe bobbed and danced. Now he could see the level stretch of white sand beach below the walls of the fort. It was dotted thickly with the lodges of hundreds of Indian families. That would be his landing.

"Macatebinessi," Father Baraga said to the Indian in the bow, "there are many Chippewas now from the great lake to the north. Will you know some of them, perhaps?"

The two Indians plied their paddles with increased caution.

Macatebinessi, "Blackbird," turned his head ever so slightly to say over his shoulder: "We shall wait and see. Many of them stop at Sault Ste. Marie. There are fine fish in the swift water there."

Wabisagime ("White Mosquito"), paddling steadily at the stern, said, "They do not speak just as we do, Nosse.* And they are very bad, too. They do not love God as you have taught us to do."

"No," Blackbird responded without turning, "I know good men among them. We are Ottawas and they are Ojibways.** But they are our brothers, Nosse."

"Well spoken, my good Blackbird," the missionary returned. "Yes, they are our brothers, rich or poor, good or bad. Do you not see that this is true, White Mosquito?"

"Yes, Nosse, it is true. I am sorry."

The canoe pitched wildly.

"Show you are sorry with your paddle then!" Blackbird shouted back.

The canoe steadied and skimmed forward again. Smiling faintly, the priest murmured, "My children!"

As they neared the beach, they were aware that their arrival had been noticed. Scores of idling Indians had come down close to the water, where they stood waiting. Boys ran out from the shore, splashing and whooping with showy bravado. Women and girls stood aloof, intently curious. All watched, but with no offer of assistance, while the priest waded with his luggage to the dry sand. He set his burden down, and looked into the stolid faces that were like a wall before him.

---

*Nosse: Ottawa and Chippewa Indian generally for "Father" as the address for a priest.

**Ojibway and Chippewa are synonymous terms.

"Boo-zou,* Nosse!" The wall disintegrated and they crowded up to shake his hand. It was evident that most of them knew him.

"I come now from Arbre Croche,"** he told them simply. He saw many, adults and children, whom he had baptized at Manistique, at Beaver Island, and in all the vicinity of the Traverse bays.

An old man came shambling forward.

"God bless you, Southern Bird," the missionary exclaimed. "You are far from home. I saw you last on the Grand River!† Tell me, how are my children at that far place?"

"Nosse, your children on the Grand River long for you," the old Indian told him, shaking his head sadly.

"But you shall carry back a message to them, Southern Bird."

"Messages are only leaves that fall on the ground. The strong wind blows them away."

Father Baraga laid his hand on the old man's shoulder. "The seeds fall with the leaves, Southern Bird. Many of them spring to life and grow large and strong. We shall talk tomorrow. Point out your lodge so that I may find it. Now I have some business in the town."

They watched him stoop to pick up his belongings and struggle through the loose, dry sand of the upper littoral, bent by his burden. None offered to carry it. Even Blackbird and White Mosquito, having beached the canoe, stood with the others and watched.

"He looks like one of our blood himself," a tall Ottawa said

---

*Boo-zou: the friendly greeting of all Great Lakes Indians.
**Now Harbor Springs, Michigan.
†Now Grand Rapids, Michigan.

[17]

to those about him. "I remember when his skin was very pale. Now he too is an Indian!"

"He is a good man," spoke another. There was a universal grunt of agreement.

"Much Indian. Very small good man," still another remarked.

The priest trudged along the rutted roadway toward the town. A two-wheeled cart drawn by a single horse forced him to step aside. The lazy animal stopped and the driver suddenly awakened.

"*O mon Dieu, c'est Père Baraga!*" he cried, seeing the priest. He climbed down rapidly. "Put down the portmanteau, the valise. I will take them in the cart and bring them wherever you wish. Put them down at once, mon Père!"

"They are not very heavy, Jean," the priest smiled. But Jean had seized the luggage and was already stowing it carefully in the cart.

"Well, you are a very stubborn man, Jean. But since you have them, will you be so kind as to leave them at Mr. Ramsey Crooks' office?"

"That I will, indeed!" Jean bowed, his cap in his hand. "And there will be Mass, mon Père? Surely! And there is another baby to be baptized."

"All will be arranged, my good Jean. Word will be given and you may help pass it along among the faithful. Your family — they are well? That is good. *Au revoir.*"

He walked on along the road more quickly now. Ahead, the little town with its neat, close-set buildings appeared like a metropolis to him. Off to his left opened the blue expanse of the straits. At his right the fort loomed, high on its bluff; he could see the mouth of a cannon through the opening in the

Mount Mary College
LIBRARY 35565

thick wall, and a sentry passing to and fro on his short round. The red, white and blue of the flag tugging in the fresh wind at the tip of the tall, straight flagpole, were vivid in the clear sunlight.

When he entered the little street the settlement seemed quite deserted. The great, rambling building of the American Fur Company dominated the whole town, the narrow street seemingly narrower still in contrast to the large expanse of white façade.

Father Baraga mounted the few steps to the wide portico, crossed to the door of the general store, and entered. After the bright sunlight, the murk within made him hesitate a moment. The air was thick with the odors of many things, mingled and blended — the scent of calico, the pungency of tobacco, the heavy breath of spirits, the mustiness of cellars, and over all, the predominating smell of undressed furs.

A young man, dapper in vest and shirt sleeves, received his message and disappeared to acquaint Mr. Ramsey Crooks with the name of his visitor. Meanwhile, Jean clattered in with the luggage, which the polite clerk, returning, took in charge.

"Mr. Crooks directs me to show you to his office at once," he told Father Baraga.

Through the door into a long narrow hallway, through another door, across an accounting room and out into another corridor they went. Here the priest noticed that his usher moved on tiptoe. He smiled, reflecting that the moccasins on his own feet were soundless enough. Now at a final door the clerk paused obsequiously and looked at him. His meaning was as plain as though he had spoken: "You are about to enter the innermost sanctum of the revered headquarters of the great American Fur Company."

Opening the door, he stepped aside and bowed the visitor in. Ramsey Crooks was seated at his desk but he arose quickly and came forward with hand outstretched.

"Father Baraga, your visit honors us!"

"I'm afraid not all fur traders would agree with you, Mr. Crooks," the missionary replied, smiling.

Ramsey Crooks seated his guest in one of the stiff office chairs and returned to his desk.

"Let me see," he said, "it is two years or more since I last saw you. You come now from Little Traverse?"

"Yes, but I had only a brief sojourn there. I come really from the Grand River and more lately from Detroit."

"And where are you bound for?"

"Lake Superior. La Pointe, if possible."

The merchant folded his arms across his chest and looked keenly at his guest. After a moment he said, "I believe you will be quite alone in that great territory, Father."

"That is why I go."

"Well," Ramsey Crooks observed, "you are a considerable traveler, Father Baraga." He let his arms fall. "It is probably five hundred miles to La Pointe. That is rather far even for an outpost. We have an establishment there, of course. But in the interior, west of the lake, are some pretty bad Indians. We have had robbery and murder to deal with up there."

"That, too, is why I go."

"Look here, Father. You were nicely established at Arbre Croche and the Indians wanted you to stay. But you went to the Grand River. Now that you have become well settled there, you're going to Lake Superior."

"Do not you merchants do the same?" Father Baraga asked.

"Oh yes," Ramsey Crooks replied, "but our motives are different. We are looking for profit."

"Just so," the priest told him. "I too am looking for profit. I am seeking the most profitable thing on earth — the conversion and redemption of a human soul. But I detain you, Mr. Crooks. My visit, after all, is on business."

"No, no, not at all!" Ramsey Crooks replied. "I am not so busy that I can't talk with you. And I see you so seldom." He arose and walked over to a wall cabinet opposite his desk. Presently he was placing a decanter and glasses on a small table. "I don't indulge often, Father," he said.

"And I, never," the missionary told him. "I thank you for your hospitality, nevertheless, Mr. Crooks."

"But Father Baraga, unless I am mistaken, we had a pleasant glass together, you and I, here in my office some years back."

"That is true, sir. And all my life, as far back as I can remember, I used the wines of our Illyria in moderation. But an experience on the Grand River persuaded me to forego utterly what had once been a mild and innocent pleasure."

"Is that so?" the merchant exclaimed. "Tell me about it." He returned the liquor service to the cabinet.

"I will tell you about it," Father Baraga assented, "though I don't like to recall it. When you greeted me here a moment ago, I remarked that not all fur traders would welcome me so cordially. I was thinking then of the Grand River. I left Arbre Croche, my first station in America, and went to the Grand River in the early summer of 1833. I suppose no missionary ever had a better place than my Arbre Croche. I had come there from Cincinnati in the spring of 1831 with Bishop Fenwick. We stopped here, if you recall, Mr. Crooks."

"Yes, indeed! I told the Bishop that his new priest from Europe wouldn't survive the first winter in the wilderness." He chuckled.

Father Baraga smiled and continued. "It was most pleasant at Arbre Croche. During those two years I went several times to the Indians at Manistique and Beaver Island and all through that vicinity. I baptized hundreds of men, women and children. We had our school. I learned the language so well that I was able to compose an Indian prayerbook — with some hymns in it, too. My Indians were so good, so tractable! We built a church. Some of my boys went to Cincinnati to learn trades. Then my bishop found it possible to relieve me at that station and I went south to the Grand River."

"Yes, I heard from some of the Indians that you had moved."

"It was very different on the Grand River," the missionary went on. "I found a Mr. Campeau living there with his family. He was kind and helpful. But the Indians were obdurate, and they were made more so by some unscrupulous traders who persisted in giving them whiskey. I don't want to be misunderstood, Mr. Crooks. I am abroad upon these lakes for the single purpose of bringing pagans to God. I am not here to interfere with merchants and traders. I do not go to them to offer opinions and counsels. But when I have baptized a pagan Indian and am leading him along the way to eternal salvation, he must not be debauched and his soul returned to darkness, nor his family be made to suffer, by those who play on his passion for whiskey. Even then I do not chide the trader who debauches him. My mission is with the Indian himself. But this some of the traders on the Grand River did not like.

[22]

"Thus it came about that they conspired to drive me away. They gave me an opportunity to remove myself and when I did not do so, they decided to get rid of me. Well, they tried for a long time, and finally one night they furnished whiskey to a large number of pagan Indians and instigated an attack upon my life."

"Impossible!" Ramsey Crooks cried.

"It is true, Mr. Crooks. That was a terrifying night. I bolted the door of my little house against a mob of drunken and infuriated Indians bent on killing me. They yelled their blood-curdling threats and battered at my door. Had they been sober, they doubtless could have broken in readily. From nightfall to dawn that howling mob surrounded me. It was then that I resolved that if it was the will of God to spare me, I would forego forever any taste of intoxicating drink. That explains why I declined your thoughtful act of hospitality, sir."

The merchant rose to his feet and walked over to the window. Suddenly he turned back to his guest, his face dark with anger. "Whiskey is a blight, a curse, a judgment of God upon the fur trade! In these cellars and warehouses at this moment are hundreds of barrels of the damnable stuff. If I could do it — if I had half the heart that beats beneath that cross upon your breast — I would take an axe and smash those barrels today." Ramsey Crooks sat down heavily. "It is the ancient curse upon us — as ancient as the fur trade itself — French, English and American. The Jesuits saw it two hundred years ago.

"And yet I cannot stop something that has been going on for two hundred years. The Indians beg our employees for whiskey at every trading station, and when they get it they are besotted for days, they neglect their hunting and fishing, they quarrel and even kill. The trade is unlawful. It was prohibited by

France and then by England, and now it is prohibited by the United States, but the arm of none of those governments has been long enough yet to enforce the ban in this upper lake country. If my company should refuse to furnish whiskey to the Indians, scores of small, independent traders, many of them unlicensed, would see that they got it. Then the furs would go to those traders and my company would soon be forced out of business."

"Man is perverse and the number of the foolish is legion," the missionary said.

"Tell me, Father, why do men go on day after day doing things that hurt them? Why does the human race go on century after century doing things that men universally condemn? Why?"

Father Baraga smiled. "My good friend, you do not really expect an answer from a poor missionary here on the edge of the American wilderness *anno Domini* 1835? I am just a simple priest, not even a reformer. We speak of whiskey in the fur trade: it is but one of an infinite number of wrongs in a wicked world. No man will enter the kingdom of heaven merely because he does not drink or trade whiskey. But when a man begins to respect himself and his fellow-men for the sole reason that man is made in the image of God, he begins, I think, to approach the answer to your question."

"Yes, of course, you are right, Father," said Ramsey Crooks. "Business never sees beyond the end of its nose. And I am one of those shortsighted businessmen who know nothing of morality."

"Well, Mr. Crooks, I am here on a business errand," the priest replied, smiling.

[24]

"Then let us proceed to deal!" was the answer in the same spirit.

"I have come to inquire about transportation to La Pointe for myself and my simple belongings."

The merchant nodded. "We have built a ship this season — it will be the only vessel on Lake Superior. I think you might take passage on it."

"It sails from here? And when?"

"No, not from here, Father. You will understand when you see the rapids at Sault Ste. Marie. We had to build her above them. It has been quite an undertaking. I bought the timbers and planking in Ohio. Prime oak, you know. We had first to get it up here to the lakes, then carry it above the rapids and build our ship there. She's a fine, sturdy little schooner of about a hundred and thirty tons. We've named her the 'John Jacob Astor' for the founder of our company."

"Will she sail soon?"

"Not for a few days. We have had to take her cargo up from here and carry all of it past the rapids. But if you want to go up the lake before she is ready, why, of course, we have dispatch canoes which travel fast and hard. I believe you would find the voyage much more pleasant on the 'Astor,' however. I will give you a letter to her master, Captain Stanard."*

"And the passage rate is how much, Mr. Crooks?"

"Why, God bless you, Father, not a shilling!"

"You are very kind."

"How do you propose to get from here to Sault Ste. Marie?"

"I suppose it will be possible to find some Indians traveling that way?" inquired Father Baraga.

---

*This navigator was the discoverer of Stannard Rock, which bears his name spelt a little differently.

"Yes, that is likely," Ramsey Crooks told him. "If you wish, you may go up on one of our boats at any time. But I know you — you will choose your Indians! At any rate, Captain Stanard will sail in the first good weather after he is fitted and loaded."

Father Baraga rose. "Now, with your leave, I shall go, Mr. Crooks. There are people seeking me. You have been very kind."

The merchant shook his hand warmly. "When shall I see you again, Father?"

"I do not know — it will be a long time, I fear."

"Well, I shall think about you up there at La Pointe," said the other sincerely. "And I don't mind telling you I'm glad our new vessel will have a man like you aboard on her first trip. It's a good omen."

CHAPTER II

ABOARD the "John Jacob Astor," Father Baraga regretted more than once that he had not chosen the alternative of a dispatch canoe. Adverse winds and calms followed by sudden violent summer storms combined to delay them or drive the ship out of her course. Also, she was on her maiden voyage, and though Captain Stanard was obviously a capable master, he had yet to learn her ways and whims. Now he humored her.

Nevertheless, the missionary sometimes forgot his impatience at the delay. There were hours of quiet contemplation on deck, where he often sat alone. At other times Captain Stanard joined him and the two had long talks.

Recollections of many things the Indians on the lower lakes had told him, his own perusal of the *Jesuit Relations* and his conversations with the ship's master built a background against which Father Baraga could place himself, as he journeyed westward on the single vessel plying this enormous lake.

In that summer of 1835 the Lake Superior country was as undeveloped with respect to its enormous and varied natural resources as it had been when the first white man beheld it. Except for one item. And that single item, furs, had by this time been exploited almost to the point of exhaustion. Yet in the very course of exploitation the Lake Superior country had accumulated a full, rich and romantic history extending across two centuries.

The physical geography of the North American continent being what it is, the first trade lines of the fur industry were laid down far to the north. The French penetrated the interior from their bases on the St. Lawrence River by the easiest water routes they could find. Thus it was that of the two peninsulas that were to form the state of Michigan, that to the north — the southern shore of Lake Superior — was well known to Europeans before any white man had visited the south peninsula. Sault Ste. Marie is a century older than Detroit.

One day Father Baraga said to Captain Stanard: "Captain, I have been thinking about this lake and the country around it. Do you know that it is an *old* new country? Strange expression, but it is true. It is old in the sense that the governments that claimed it have known it for two centuries. It is new in the sense that it remains quite uninhabited* and its resources, except fur, are undiscovered."

"You are right, Father. But there is one thing I think they will discover one of these days, and that is copper. The Indians have made small articles from it for as far back as their history goes, I guess. I am not a book man, you know; I learn these things from what I see and hear."

"Yes, the Jesuits speak of copper and other minerals in their *Relations*," Father Baraga told him. "Etienne Brule was on Lake Superior in 1616 and Jean Nicolet saw it a few years afterward. That was long before the English had settled any colony except Virginia."

"Well, the Americans have got the country now for certain, and they are descended from the English settlers. But the white men who live up here are still pretty nearly all French — and most of 'em have Indian blood in 'em now. The Americans never went in for that kind of thing much, nor the English either — marrying Indian women, I mean, and getting to live more or less like Indians. The French didn't seem to care about laying claim to the land — just fell right in with the natives, come day, go day. But the Americans, why, they want the land and everything on it and in it — except the Indians. They don't want the Indians."

"No, I am afraid they don't want the Indians," the missionary agreed.

"You know, Father, I met a Frenchman this summer at the Sault — a real book-learned Frenchman he was. He spoke some English, so we could visit with each other. One day he brought me to a place along the rapids and took a piece of paper out of

---

*The French who came in with the fur trade were nomadic and not considered settlers in any real sense.

[28]

his pocket and read it out loud in French — waved his arms a
good deal while he was doing it. When he finished I says,
'What was that?' He says, 'Captain, that was one of the great
jokes of history!' And he laughed — laughed good and hard.
Finally he hands me the paper and says, 'Here, Captain, take
this paper and keep it. Your descendants will enjoy it.' If you
will wait a minute, Father, I'll get the paper. Maybe you can
tell me what it says — it's French writing."

In a moment Captain Stanard returned and handed a paper
to Father Baraga. The priest glanced through the writing and
smiled.

"I think, Captain, your French friend had a sense of humor,"
he said. Thereupon he translated for the other's benefit:

At this spot St.-Lusson, a Cavalier of France, unfurled a
banner emblazoned with the lilies of the Bourbons, raised
his sword in a graceful gesture, stepped forward and spoke
the following words: "In the name of the Most High, Most
Mighty and Redoubtable Monarch, Louis XIV, of the
name, Most Christian King of France and Navarre, we take
possession of said place of St. Mary's of the Falls, as well as
Lakes Huron and Superior, the Manitoulin Islands, and of
all other countries, rivers, lakes and tributaries contiguous,
as well discovered as to be discovered, which are bounded
on the one side by the northern and western seas and on the
other side by the south sea, including all its length and
breadth."

Smiling, he handed the paper back to the captain.

"Well, I'll be — blest!" the latter exclaimed, looking down
at the writing. "No wonder the fellow laughed!"

"Captain," Father Baraga said, "it seems to me that I can
sit here now and see in one direction the retreating figures of an

old regime, and in the opposite direction the on-rushing vanguard of a new regime. I see both of them clearly. It has been as though these great waters and their environs have been sleeping for two hundred years. On my way here I saw those restless Americans on the Ohio River; they were crowding the wharves in Detroit just after they had come in through the Erie Canal. They were tall, stalwart men and with them were their wives and their children and their cattle and their household goods. That French cavalier made one historical gesture when he thrust the staff of the Bourbon flag into the ground at his feet, but each of these Americans will be making quite another kind of historical gesture when he thrusts his spade into the earth. God be merciful to my poor Indians!"

"Yes, things are going to change," agreed Captain Stanard.

When Father Baraga was alone once more, he thought: It has been a century and a half since Allouez and Marquette were on Lake Superior. I wonder if I shall find at that Pointe du Saint Esprit that Allouez named, any vestige of their work?

He recalled now what he had learned during his first months in America, while he waited at Cincinnati for Bishop Fenwick to take him to his mission station at Arbre Croche. Allouez had been at La Pointe for four years, beginning in his restless endeavor what Marquette was to take over for a year or two until he departed to join Joliet in the expedition that explored the Upper Mississippi River. Marquette was at La Pointe in 1669, and now Frederic Baraga was succeeding him in 1835; for no priest had been there in the interim.

How much of what Allouez and Marquette saw on this lake has changed by now? he wondered. If I am to rely upon what my Indians below here have told me, then the end of the fabulous fur trade is near. And though all the motions of that old regime are still being made, nevertheless a period is ending. Am I to inherit all the accumulated ills that it has brought these Indians?

Day followed day in seemingly endless succession. Even Captain Stanard grew fretful when he was compelled to turn and run before a storm. On that occasion only the immensity of the lake gave them the sea-room necessary to save the little schooner.

Finally, on the eighteenth day after they had left the Sault, the master announced, "Father, if all goes well we should make a landing at La Pointe some time between daybreak and noon tomorrow."

"Deo gratias!" murmured the priest from his heart.

CHAPTER III

THE Wisconsin land mass thrusts a blunt peninsula into the far western end of Lake Superior to form a notable feature of the south shore of the great lake. The early French explorers named it La Pointe du St. Esprit, which became commonly "La Pointe." The Indians used the name Chequamegon to identify the region, which was one of their two important centers of more or less permanent abode, the other being Sault Ste. Marie.

Just off the peninsula is an archipelago known as the Apostle Islands, the chief of them being Madeline Island. To this the Indians finally removed from the sites they originally occupied on the mainland, probably because the island offered a superior defense in their long war with the westward Sioux. The name La Pointe then came to be applied exclusively to the settlement on Madeline Island, to which Father Baraga was to come in 1835.

The American Fur Company's "factory" at La Pointe was an orderly cluster of neat buildings under a hot July sun. High overhead the flag hung limply at the top of the tall spruce pole. The two large store buildings glistened in their white paint, unrelieved by any shade of living tree. But along the narrow street beyond, where small cottages stood close together on either side behind whitewashed picket fences, trees cast a dense shade. From the slight eminence on which the buildings were crowded a cart road ran down briefly to a wharf lined with long, squat warehouses; these had been colored the austere dun with which nature paints the natural wood in the Lake Superior country.

From somewhere within this row of warehouses sounds of hammering began, and this monotonous rhythm was occasionally punctuated by the sharper noise of lumber being moved about.

This single and sudden evidence of human activity brought two immediate consequences in its train. A corpulent Indian who had been sleeping in the shade cast by the warehouses roused himself, listened until he had identified the source of this industry, slouched along the wharf to the shade farthest removed from the noises, and stretching full length on the planking, resumed his midday slumbers.

The second consequence was the appearance, at the entrance of one of the store buildings, of Dr. Borup, the factor. This gentleman, notwithstanding that his movements were energetic,

apparently was in no hurry. He walked to the foot of the flagpole and stood there looking down upon the dock and warehouses. Then he looked up the little lane faced by the neat
white cottages behind their picket fences. He removed his hat
and peered straight up the flagpole at the limp emblem. Then
he returned his hat to his head and turned about to inspect the
façade of the store building. All these things he did very
methodically as though he had stepped out of his office for that
purpose. Now he seemed to remember a paper that he carried
in his hand, and studied it for a moment. When he looked up
again, his gaze fell far off upon the horizon of sky and lake,
and he scanned this intently. At last he moved his head in a
negative gesture and began the descent that led to the wharf.
Though his was the single moving figure on the scene, Dr.
Borup's progress gave the impression of a solemn and dignified
procession, as if some invisible retinue accompanied him.

He headed straight for that part of the warehouses whence
the sounds of hammering came.

When the factor entered the cooper's shop, old Joseph
Dufault laid down his drawknife, spoke one word to his hammering helper and brushed the shavings from his leather apron.
Sweat beaded his forehead, so he took time to wipe it away
with the sleeve of his bright calico shirt. These were the ges-
tures of preparation for his reception of the factor; now he
stood at his place before the bench watching the slow approach
of the great man from the fort, as the Company buildings on
the hill were generally called.

Dr. Borup was in no hurry. He picked his way among the
lumber that littered the floor, stopping after every two or three
steps to look about. He surveyed the row of finished casks
along one wall. He inspected an unfinished barrel, exploring

[33]

the workmanship with his hand. He stooped to pick up a stave from the floor, lifting and lowering it to judge its weight, and holding the clean wood close under his nose to sniff before discarding it.

When he stood before old Joseph at last, he looked into the cooper's face for some moments while a quizzical smile gathered on his own.

"Joseph, do you think you can build a church?"

The old man brushed his calloused hands together in a quick gesture.

"Like dat!" he replied. Then he threw back his head with a cackling laugh. "*Oui,* Doctaire, I buil' *la chapelle* so easy as I buil' the barrel. Like dat!" He brushed off his hands in another quick dismissing movement.

But suddenly the laughing old face changed. He set his jaws together so that his nose and his chin almost met, and his eyes narrowed as he studied Dr. Borup's face. He spoke no question but the factor felt compelled to answer the keenly inquiring look. Dr. Borup brushed off a space on the bench and hoisted himself up to sit there. He still carried the paper in his hand and now he looked at it thoughtfully.

"Joseph, what would you say if I told you a ship was on her way here? A real ship, Joseph — a schooner with masts and sails? Now, now, now — just a moment! And what would you say if I told you that this ship is bringing a priest to La Pointe?"

A quick light shone momentarily in the old cooper's eyes but he waited for the other to continue.

"Well, but answer! What would you say, Joseph?"

"The ship — *oui,* that I might believe. But *le père?* Nevaire!"

"Well, you had better believe it for it is true!"

[34]

"O Doctaire, from *La Belle* — "

"Oh, no, no, no, Joseph!" The factor had seen an expression of wistful wonder flit across the old man's face. "No, I'm afraid you can't have everything, Joseph. A priest, yes. But not from your *'Belle Montreal!'* "

Dr. Borup brought the paper in his hand up into reading position. *"B-a-r-a-g-a.* Wait now, one of the clerks at Mackinac has explained how to say it. Yes, here it is. 'I will explain how to say the name. The first part is neither *bar* nor *bare* but something right in between. The accent is on that part. The *g* is given the hard sound.' So that's the name, Joseph. Let's attempt to say it now. I make it *Bahr'-a-gah.* Yes, that will do nicely, I think. Now try it, Joseph, for you will want to greet him by his name when he arrives."

Joseph repeated the syllables after the factor, who approved with a nod. But then the old man's face assumed a puzzled expression and he slowly shook his head.

"I do not know dat name," he said.

"Nor I," the factor admitted. "But never mind — Mr. Crooks speaks of him as his friend. This came by dispatch canoe." He shook the paper in his hand. "Now, Joseph, do you suppose you can build a church?"

Joseph Dufault's face took on an eager wistfulness that astonished the factor. The old man's gnarled hands were clasped before him and tears ran down his wrinkled cheeks. He did not seem to see Dr. Borup — he was looking beyond him to some far vision.

"Oui," he said softly, "I buil' the boat, the house, the store, the sleigh, the barrel. I am ol' man now. I am mos' glad to buil' *la chapelle* before I die."

[35]

"Well, well, Joseph, you old people have been very patient, for a fact." Borup spoke briskly as he climbed down from the bench. "We shall see about it. We shall see."

By sundown La Pointe was very different from the somnolent place of the afternoon. Along the little picketed street women sat in their front gardens and chatted back and forth with neighbors on either side. Children occupied the lane with busy games. Men loitered about the wharf and before the fort, smoking and exchanging small talk.

At their village down along the flat beach the Indians sat about in small groups, the men taciturn and idle while the women plied their needles. In and out among them ran children at their games, and dogs were everywhere, exploring the poor prospect of scraps to assuage their perpetual hunger.

Word had been passed around that Dr. Borup would give them some news at dusk. As the light diminished the people began moving toward the flagpole, the natural meeting-place of the little community, and gradually the space before the fort filled. The Indians remained at the rim of the growing crowd, as silent as the Company women were garrulous.

But all talking ceased abruptly as the factor came forth. The crowd arranged itself in a compact arc before him, awaiting his announcement with an intentness hardly imaginable in our day of globe-spanning cables and news broadcasts.

A shrewd dealer with people, Dr. Borup reserved his news, beginning his talk with the admonition which otherwise would have gone unheeded.

"I have told you before that I am not satisfied with the fishing. No, I am not satisfied, I am provoked! There are men here who do not go out at all some days — and you women encourage them. It must stop! You know very well that the Company cannot stay here in these times for the fur trade alone. There is not enough business for that. These fisheries must be worked. Joseph Dufault has seventy empty casks on hand now and no fish to put in them.

"What are you going to do? I will not furnish provisions to men who do not work. Forty boats should have been out on the fishing grounds today and there were seven! I ask some men why they are not out and they say, 'Oh, it is too hot!' Well, let me tell you that pretty soon it will be too cold. The time to do this fishing is now while the weather is good. Some day I will say to your women when they come to the store for provisions, 'Oh, it is too hot today, I can't be bothered!' How will you like that?

"You think the Company will take care of you. Yes, it will, but only if you work. If you don't, I tell you, the Company will not remain here. This is the year 1835 and not the year 1820 when we started and furs were so plentiful.

"Now, are you there, Buffalo?" Dr. Borup raised his voice, looking at the same time over the heads of the near crowd toward the outer fringe of Indians.

"Ho!" came back a grunt from the gathering darkness.

"Very well, Buffalo. As chief of your band, you tell your men that they must fish. They go out and catch three or four fish and come in and eat them. That won't do. I asked Wahnekoace down on the wharf today why he was sleeping and not fishing. I said, 'Why do you not fish today?' He said, 'Oh, fish last sun!' I said, 'Well, Wahnekoace, if you can fish yesterday, you can eat yesterday!'"

Dr. Borup paused a long moment to let his auditors digest these salutary morsels. "Now I have a little news," he went on. "Letters came today by dispatch canoe from Mackinac. All seems to be well with our friends to the east, at Michilimackinac and St. Mary's* and L'Anse. There has been no sickness and the weather has been favorable. It is thought that the annual payment to the Indians will be held here at La Pointe in October, so they will not have to go east for it. The Indians up beyond here, around Fond du Lac and above, will come down here. A fine new ship has been built by the Company, bigger than any you have ever seen. We can expect it almost any day now. It is bringing supplies and will take cargo here. It has been named the 'John Jacob Astor.'

"And also I am pleased to tell you that a priest is coming to La Pointe on that ship. His name is Father Baraga. I do not know this Father Baraga but I am told that he has been on the lower lakes for some years. Now he has come to Lake Superior. I do not know what he will want to do about a church, but I hope he will want to build one; then all the men who do not go out to fish each day will have no excuse for idleness — they can work on the church. And I hope the Father will make them work very hard and for no pay, of course. Then I think we may get more fishing done. Good night."

Dr. Borup, chuckling at his own wit, made his way back to the fort through the darkness. He left behind him a crowd that was a little awed by the news he had given. A ship and a priest!

A small woman with an infant in her arms said aloud, *"Dieu soit bénit, un prêtre!"*

Michilimackinac: now, Mackinac; the site of Marquette's Mission of St. Ignace. *St. Mary's:* Sault Ste. Marie.

CHAPTER IV

THE "John Jacob Astor" came in under a gentle breeze, moving slowly to the wharf that was lined with an eager, noisy, gesticulating crowd. As she sidled up to the wharf with almost imperceptible motion, there was quick activity both aboard and ashore. Her lines were thrown and made fast. Men milled about in happy, boisterous confusion.

Up on the little foredeck one man stood quietly alone. No one noticed him for he was quite hidden by piled-up deck cargo. The crowd were all eyes for the first ship most of them had ever seen. They had quite forgotten for the moment the arrival of their priest.

In this excitement, Father Baraga made no attempt to disembark. He watched the noisy, exuberant voyageurs back-slapping their greetings. And beyond the milling group he scanned the immobile faces of scores of Indians who formed a stolid background.

But soon he noticed a new movement on the wharf. The crowd, suddenly quiet, had fallen back to make room for a man whom the captain was helping up to the deck. It was all managed so briskly that Father Baraga started with surprise when Captain Stanard pointed to him and he realized that he had become the center of attention, on deck and on shore.

"Father Baraga, I am Dr. Borup, the Company's factor."

Before the priest had time to greet him, Dr. Borup turned quickly to the hushed audience and raised an authoritative hand.

"He has come!" he declared. "Your priest is here at last. This is Father Baraga!"

[39]

In that still moment Frederic Baraga stepped forward. His slight, straight figure was now plainly in view. Slowly he raised his arm. At once the Canadians knelt down. He blessed them, and then greeted them in familiar French words. And when those words ended, while they were still kneeling, the priest looked over their heads upon the throng of Indians who stood impassively watching. With arm still upraised, he repeated his blessing in the Indian tongue. But no Indian knelt.

The phrases which some of the Canadians had not heard since childhood, had come to their ears in tones so gentle that, their eyes downcast, each of them seemed to feel the benign pressure of a hand laid upon his uncovered head. But the Chippewa words were familiar too, because Indian and French blood were mixed in their veins. For many of them the Indian words were more meaningful than the French. In the Indian tongue, the low, compassionate voice was like a soothing sound in nature — clear water running over stones, leaves rustling in the breeze, rain on the roof of the lodge. They were reluctant to disturb the spell the blessing had cast upon them.

But the alert eyes of the stolid Indians were fixed upon this blackrobe who spoke their tongue. They gave no outward sign of surprise but they were trying to discover in him something they had not perceived before he blessed them. They saw a small, black-robed figure without adornment of any kind except the silver cross hanging upon his breast. They saw a narrow, smooth face tanned by sun and wind, and framed in long brown hair. They saw eyes as blue as the waters of Lake Superior under the sunlight. Something surprised and caught them. When he lowered his arm and ceased speaking, a muffled and reluctant "Ho, ho!" of approval ran among them.

The wharf was lined with an eager, noisy crowd.

[41]

But now the excitement of watching the discharge of cargo caught them again. Father Baraga, who never changed his custom of speaking of the Indians as "my children," understood their mood. How could they divide their attention between a new priest, even though none had visited them within the memory of the oldest inhabitant of La Pointe, and these boxes and crates and barrels now being trundled from the boat into the warehouses? They were a simple people, with the unspoiled capacity for wonder that went with their time and place. Their very children, who, entirely naked, were dodging in and out among the moving freight while one of the Company clerks scurried after them, were hardly more full of curiosity.

The Canadians were sweating, ribald, vociferous under their tasks. Even Dr. Borup and Captain Stanard were engaged now. Thus the missionary found it easy to walk away from the wharf and inspect this place that was to be his home.

He climbed the slope under the hot sun and followed the little road to the upper ground. Turning then and looking down upon the busy scene, he could see far beyond to the open water he had traversed. The schooner looked tiny in that great perspective. He turned landward again.

This, he knew, would be the "fort" of which Captain Stanard had spoken. He looked down the white-picketed street and thought these little homes behind the fences were pleasant and clean. He saw log houses beyond, and Indian lodges, thrice the number of the houses, along the beach below.

There was nothing strange to him in what he saw. Yet, standing here alone, he knew there was a difference. It is so vast a country, he thought. So vast a country, inhabited by so few and such poor people. As he glanced out over Lake Superior and thought of the many days the little ship had fought its way toward this far place, a sense of that vastness almost over-whelmed him.

What would they think in Vienna now, he wondered, if they could see me standing in this spot? And that reminds me — their Leopoldine Society votes me some funds for a mission among the American Indians. Very well, let me inspect the con-dition of those funds inasmuch as I have finally arrived at my destination. From beneath his robe he brought forth a small purse. He opened it and smiled ruefully. Inside were three American dollars. A mission to a poor people by a poorer priest!

He bowed his head a moment and then lifted it to look straight out upon the lake. It had been that immensity of water which had given him the momentary constriction of fear. Have I merely transferred myself from wretchedness to stark misery? he asked himself. These are a poorer people than I have ever known. I have yet to erect a church. I have yet to find means of traveling through all this endless country. I have no col-league with whom I might confer. I have no roof, even. And I have three dollars in my pocket.

He turned away from the little plaza before the fort, ignored the bustling activity upon the wharf, and bent his steps toward an Indian lodge in the distance where an old woman sat nod-ding in the sun.

CHAPTER V

Dr. BORUP said, "I have a letter from Mr. Crooks, sent by the boat. It is possible, I suppose, for us to give you some assistance."

Father Baraga stood with the factor in the little street where they had just encountered each other. The priest had made no mention of his desire to build a church.

"I had not expected any help from the Company, Dr. Borup," he now said. "Perhaps a few small items to be paid for at a later time. But I need not say how grateful I am for your good will. Now, will you be so kind as to tell me who among the people here can give practical advice — who is qualified by skill and experience to direct the work?"

"That would be Joseph Dufault," the factor replied. "Come, I will take you to him."

None of the men in the local hierarchy of the American Fur Company was a communicant of Father Baraga's Church; Dr. Borup went to some trouble to make that clear to him. On the other hand, all the Company's employees with any degree of white blood were attached to that Faith — in varying degrees. Borup thought he could read what was in the mind of Ramsey Crooks between the lines of his letter. He himself was convinced that it might be good business to give some gesture of assistance. The priest's presence here might make the men more contented and generally insure to the Company better service from them. As for the Indians, if the priest was not meddlesome, if he did not interfere with the policy long ago adopted, then certainly their conversion to some form of Christian worship would probably have a quieting influence and make them generally easier to deal with.

That day building plans were made for the church. There was no drawing. By word and gesture the priest and the builder developed their ideas of its architecture and design, until each could see the completed edifice clearly in his mind. The result, when desirabilities were reconciled with actualities, was a projected building about fifty feet long and half as wide, with walls a score of feet high.

Dr. Borup was astonished, but he did not feel called upon to demonstrate his astonishment. He thought: Why, this fellow has no ambitious plans. How unpretentious his church will be! And he talks as though he expected to go to work on it himself. I am afraid these people will take advantage of him; he won't know how to handle them. Never mind, I will look out for him.

"Now, mon Père, you know what place she go?"

"No, Joseph, I have not thought yet of the site. In that matter, Dr. Borup will have to be consulted."

"Well, now, I hadn't given it any thought either," Dr. Borup admitted. "But I'll tell you, Joseph: suppose you go with Father Baraga and look around and the two of you decide. You will want it a little way from the fort but not too far. Wherever you decide will be all right, but let me know the spot after you have picked it out."

Zealous though he was, Father Baraga was overwhelmed by the rush of activity that followed the selection of a site for the new church. There were timbers to be brought to the grounds and framed there under the watchful eye of Joseph Dufault. Straight pieces fifty feet long were hewed and laid one atop another to make the walls. Never had the priest known men so dexterous with the axe. Each log was rolled slowly while old

[45]

Joseph squinted along it to catch the straightest side. Then a wave of his hand indicated his decision.

"Now you, Baptiste," or "Now, Alexis," or "You, Jean," he would say, and the axes would sink deep along the sides of the log as the old man directed. After this scoring, the round sides fell away under the deft axe-strokes, so that clean, flat, smooth surfaces finally appeared. Watching, Father Baraga heard the soft grunts of the workers as the air was forced from their lungs by the mighty swinging of their arms. When they sat panting on the timbers and sweat poured from their bodies, he would walk among them, saying not a word but sometimes letting his hand rest for a moment on their strong shoulders.

While they rested, they lighted their pipes and talked.

"Dat is le bon wood, mon Père, dat spruce," Baptiste offered at one interval of rest. He picked up a long, clean chip, smelled of it, chewed on it contemplatively. "Clean, by gar!"

"It is good wood," Father Baraga agreed, seating himself on a timber near the men.

"Clean, by gar — no lak dat 'Balm a' Gilead'! Faugh!"

"I don't believe I know that wood you speak of, Baptiste. You call it 'Balm of Gilead'?"

Instantly he perceived that all eyes were looking at him in astonishment.

"I don't know that tree," he repeated. "Can you show me one hereabouts? Or can you bring me a piece of the wood, Baptiste?"

It was clearly evident now that the moment was embarrassing to all the men sitting near him.

"No! I nevaire put my han' on dat wood!" Baptiste exclaimed. And he made a quick gesture of crossing himself. All the others were very quiet, looking upon the ground. Father

Baraga, feeling the tension in the group, struggled against a secret annoyance.

"Very well, Baptiste!" he smiled. "Now your Père must learn. Please tell me, what is bad about that wood?"

Old Joseph Dufault spoke now. He sat opposite Father Baraga and now leaned forward to peer into his face.

"Don' you know, mon Père, dat da Cross was mak' of dat wood?"

The priest knew then that he had quite innocently failed these childlike souls. He realized in that sudden moment that some essence of their simple faith had been shown to him. He did not utter his first thought: that he knew of no historical proof of their statement. The superstition in their attitude offended him. But underneath was faith — they felt so because they believed. Now, he thought, this is the beginning! It is from here that I must start, not to destroy but to teach and lead.

He raised his eyes and searched their faces, one at a time, from end to end of the line of men sitting before him on the timber. Then his eyes returned to Baptiste, and he smiled.

"You see, you teach your priest, my good Baptiste! So it is in the world. All about us here is good and bad wood. There are many good trees and some bad trees. Baptiste tells us that is true. So I tell you, my dear children, that everywhere in the world are many good and many bad things. Each of us must learn, each one for himself, which are the good and which the bad, even as I now have learned from Baptiste. And now let us get on with our work!"

Then, one day, in the neat little steeple that Joseph Dufault had trusted only himself to build, a small bell was hung. It had been cast in Detroit on Father Baraga's order and Ramsey Crooks had had it forwarded to La Pointe. It was incredible:

nine days after the arrival of the missionary, here was a little church in the wilderness!

"Humph, well," said Dr. Borup to himself as he stood and surveyed the new building, "I must say that priest needs no looking after. He's got more work out of some of them in nine days than I can get in nine months. I will suggest, with great tact, of course, that he persuade them to get out on the fishing grounds now that the church is built. I'll look him up at once. Now where the deuce does the man live, anyway? I've forgotten to ask. Where did he find room, I wonder?"

The factor found his man in an abandoned and dilapidated log cabin on the outskirts of the settlement. Father Baraga was cooking a pot of whitefish and potatoes over a little fire outdoors, Indian fashion.

It mattered nothing to the missionary that he had lacked a suitable dwelling during the summer. Had he not a church? Yet the new house appeared almost as swiftly that autumn as the church had a few weeks earlier. One room was designed as a schoolroom, in which, whenever he could, he would gather the children.

The church was built on a site known to the old inhabitants as "Middlefort." For it was an ancient settlement, this La Pointe. The Northwest Company had had a fort there long before the American Fur Company displaced it, though by now all evidences of the existence of Middlefort had been obliterated by the slow, relentless creeping back of the forest to repossess what man had briefly taken from it. Thus the new church was some little distance from the present fort. This had been Father Baraga's desire from the beginning.

It befell that the church was ready to be blessed on the feast of St. Joseph Calasanctius, so it was given St. Joseph's name.

There was a holiday at La Pointe. The clear, thin tones of the little bell floated over the wilderness silence, small, brave and strange. A procession was formed at the fort to march to the church. The Canadian families, dressed in their best, were first in the line, each head of a family shepherding his own. These men walked proudly. Had not each of them with his own hands helped to erect this holy edifice, and was he not now leading his children there to worship in the religion of his fathers?

Nor did any of the Indians on the island remain away. Impressed by the sound of the bell, they caught the spirit of the occasion from the Canadians.

Only a small part of the throng could find room inside the church. The double doors were left open and those without, quiet and curious, caught glimpses of the altar, saw the deliberate movements of the priest, and heard the low but clear tones of his voice.

After the celebration of Mass, Father Baraga requested those within to join those outside. Standing on the step of the church before the open door, he addressed the Indians. He chose the Chippewa tongue because all those present understood it. In the simplest words he could muster, he told them of his sojourn on the lakes below, of how he had learned their language in order that he might help them, of his desire to live among them so that he might teach them of the goodness of God. They listened with rapt attention. But when he had finished and stood silent before them, they turned and walked solemnly away.

Father Baraga took stock of his situation. There were in the settlement two wholly white families, and sixty-five families of mixed blood. The heads of these families were attached, more or less, to the Company as employees. Their scale of living,

[49]

poor enough indeed, was markedly better than that of the Indians. They lived in small but comfortable log houses. In the commercial activities of the Company there was considerable division of labor and the nature of the employment fixed the economic and social position of the man and his family. There were clerks in the store; there were clerks and voyageurs who traveled far away from La Pointe in season; there were men who labored in the extensive fisheries operated by the Company; and there were a few artisans.

These were a friendly, happy, generous and irresponsible people. They had their small ambitions, nursed their little prides, performed their religious duties, sometimes with great enthusiasm, sometimes not at all. To these he ministered with patience and admonishment, as needed. However, it was not these who had brought him to the rigors of Lake Superior.

Through the late summer and early autumn days, he visited the Indian village again and again. He observed with deep pity the extreme poverty and economic helplessness evident everywhere. He saw the naked children, noted the insufficiency of food and sensed the despair and hopelessness of these native people. Only a few of the many hundreds of these Indians would remain at La Pointe during the winter — their hunting would take them far into the interior along the waters of the Brule, the St. Croix, the St. Louis and a score of other rivers. This summer metropolis would be deserted when cold weather had settled at last upon the great inland sea.

Experience on the lower lakes had taught him that the older men and women, and the children, were more responsive than the youths and those of early adulthood. The young braves, proud and haughty, were often insolent and quarrelsome.

Buffalo's lodge was the largest in the village, as befitted the chief. Stout saplings had been cut and forced into the ground, and their tops brought together to form an elliptical shelter. On top of the saplings sheets of cedar bark, overlapping like shingles or clapboarding, were fastened to make the roof and walls.

When Father Baraga appeared at the entrance, Buffalo was seated on a mat in the center of the floor. He was a large man, mature in years and with great dignity of bearing.

"Boo-zou," the missionary greeted him, waiting at the door.

Buffalo returned the greeting and bade him enter. The chief did not move, but ordered a woman to bring another mat for his guest.

Well did Father Baraga know that the inevitable "fumerie" awaited him. This was the ceremonial pipe-smoking that preceded all serious talk, without exception. Buffalo uttered no word until, with calculated deliberation, the pipe had been filled and lighted. Then, taking a few puffs, he handed it across to the priest who sat facing him on the guest mat. Father Baraga accepted the pipe as the gesture of friendship that was intended, took a ritual puff and returned it to the chief.

"There have been many words spoken," Buffalo began in the Chippewa tongue, "about the Great White Father at Washington wanting our lands. It is said many times that we will be moved to the country of the setting sun. But that would deliver us over to our natural enemies, the Sioux. What is this religion that our white brothers practice when they do that? What is this religion that takes our land and makes us poor and miserable?"

Buffalo ceased and his features as he looked straight into

[51]

Father Baraga's face were as cold and hard as though graven of stone.

"My brother," the priest replied, "I have heard that talk of which you speak. It makes me very sad. A winter ago I was living on the Grand River, far to the south. The Indian agent there became very angry with me. The Indians were being moved toward the setting sun and they did not want to go. I tried to help them.

"But wait, my brother, in the forest we must be very careful and look for a long time at what we see. We may think at first it is something that will harm us, and yet when we stand very still and look at it carefully, we often discover that it is not what we thought it was. I have seen a blackened stump that I at first thought was a bear.

"You ask me, 'What is this religion that cheats us?' I reply, 'That is not any religion.' As in the forest you must stand very still and look carefully for a long time, so now you must sit quietly in your lodge and look carefully for a long time at this thing you think you see. It is not religion that makes men do these things. Your white brothers are many, and they are increasing in numbers very rapidly; their old places are becoming crowded. It is really hard for them. But some, I am sorry to say, are also very greedy."

Buffalo grunted.

"I have seen an Indian eat food like a glutton because it lay before him, eat until he made himself sick. Our white brothers eat our land like gluttons."

"Yes, my brother, it is true. You are an old man who has learned much wisdom in many winters. But I ask you if you can always control your young men when they desire to do foolish things? It has always been so. Upon this earth there is much

[52]

unhappiness and misery because men are foolish. But there is another world where all is happiness and peace. It is for men like you, who have gathered great wisdom, to try to bring some of that happiness and peace into this world where we must live for a little time. If we love God with all our hearts, and all our minds, and all our souls, then for time that is without ending, we shall be happy.

"See, my brother! In a land very far from this place, across a great sea, I lived in a house as big as all the houses and lodges at La Pointe put together. I owned land as far as the eye could see. All that was mine. But I did not want it; I wanted something else. I gave it all away. If I had kept it, perhaps I would have wanted more and more land and then I would have been unhappy indeed. Oh, my brother, it is not really unhappiness to be poor. It is the greedy who are unhappy! It is very hard to see these things, as when the fog hides the shore. But I tell you that if I owned all the lands that touch this great lake, I could not be as happy as I shall be if I can teach the poorest person in your tribe to love God."

Father Baraga had talked directly to Buffalo in a low tone. He now looked earnestly into the stolid bronze face before him.

Buffalo sat a long time in silence and the priest said no more. At last the Indian sighed and spoke. "I do not know. I will think about it. But it is hard to be happy when there is nothing to eat. I think you are a good man, my brother."

He opened the school in his dwelling, teaching reading and writing. Attendance was irregular but some of the children were persistent enough to make excellent progress. These were the half- and quarter-breeds. But his especial efforts were directed toward gaining the confidence of the Indian children.

His days were full — long rounds of duties he imposed upon himself. It was at this time that he began a practice he would always maintain thereafter: he arose at four o'clock each morning and devoted two hours to Mass and prayer before breaking his fast. Besides his school, church services, baptisms, confessions, he still found time to visit the Indians from lodge to lodge, widening his acquaintance among them, pressing with gentle insistence the need of baptism that would open the way to spiritual growth.

Among the Canadians, at all events, the number of communicants grew, and by late autumn he had the added duty of hearing confessions far into the night as the men prepared themselves for the far, perilous journeys ahead of them.

One morning he discovered the "John Jacob Astor" at the wharf. This was probably her last trip, he learned, before the season of navigation closed. So that night, after he had performed his numerous offices and the last visitor had gone, he sat at a deal table in his room and penned a letter by the light of a taper.

He wrote to Amalia, saying: "I must scold you a little for giving yourself so much unnecessary worry and care; for being so much afraid, on my account, of the cold winters, the hardships, hunger and thirst, and all kinds of dangers which you think will overtake me on my travels. Do not, I beseech you, my dear sister, let these trifles worry you. Now, at this time here, all is activity in preparation for the year's commercial ventures by land and water. As merchants do not shrink from peril and hardship in order to increase the possessions which they can enjoy only to the end of their short lives, why should these difficulties frighten me who have no other object in view than to gain immortal souls to heaven?"

CHAPTER VI

FROM the time of his arrival in America, Father Baraga had written Amalia as regularly as his situation permitted. Fearing, however, to rouse her anxiety concerning his welfare and safety, he never recorded his experiences completely. Now, in attempting to describe the country merely for the purpose of enlightening her, he discovered that he had written words he could not send, and he destroyed a precious sheet of writing paper in re-forming his letter. He had written, "Truly, this is a dreary country. As early as mid-September we saw snowflakes falling, and for several weeks past house fires have been lighted." He would not tell her that the winter clothing he had ordered had not arrived. And this was the schooner's last trip of the year.

But these were incidentals, quickly swept away by his apostolic ardor. It was ninety miles to Fond du Lac and he was resolved to go there on a mission before winter set in.

Day was just breaking and a mist hung low upon the protected water in the lee of Madeline Island. Father Baraga could just discern the figure of Louis Gaudin, his voyageur, crouched on the sandy beach awaiting him. Gaudin's canoe was inverted just free of the water and the man squatted beside it, smoking and humming a low tune. There was a penetrating chill in the air and Father Baraga shivered in his thin garments. He stood beside his voyageur ready for the long journey in his black cassock, with moccasins on his feet and a three-cornered hat on his head, and no other equipment for the venture except Mass kit and breviary.

Louis flipped the canoe right side up and set it in the water. He stowed a small pack and indicated in a low voice that the missionary was to take his seat forward. When all was ready, the voyageur with one shove launched both himself and his craft. Then he was paddling and they were on their way.

They had purposely embarked behind a point of land on the far side of the island not only because it shortened the distance a little but also because it gave them the quieter water of the channels among the islands. Father Baraga, whose prayers had been interrupted by this early start, now resumed them. Gaudin was silent, paddling steadily with strong, sweeping strokes, in the immensity made vague by the mist.

As full daylight came slowly on, the mist thinned and lifted on a light breeze that soon chopped the surface into short, active waves. The canoe bobbed blithely and their progress was easily apparent by the marks they recognized along the shore.

In the forenoon Gaudin decided that it was time to eat. He brought the canoe toward a low sand beach that stretched away from a headland on which trees were growing. Skirting the flat beach, he rounded the ridge and was almost immediately in the mouth of a small river.

On the bank they quickly gathered some dry fuel and from his pouch Gaudin produced flint and steel and a piece of dry punk. Pipe and fire were soon going to his satisfaction. He took a tin kettle from the pack and deposited in it a piece of salt pork which he covered with water. The fire was small and he hung the kettle over it so that the peak of the flame touched the bottom. While the pork was cooking, he made a dough of flour and water and cut it into strips with his belt knife. After a time he tested the meat, decided it was ready, and dumped the strips of dough into the boiling kettle. Soon all was done. He took the kettle off the fire and invited the priest to partake. They ate together from the kettle, their first meal since the night before. Two meals in twenty-four hours was the usual practice en route. Sometimes tea was added.

Father Baraga was no stranger to such a meal. It was the standard voyageur cuisine on the Great Lakes. He was not squeamish but he felt no relish for the food, taking it only for the strength it would give him. His hungry companion ate with veritable ferocity, leaving not a scrap. Dinner over, the big voyageur prepared to take his ease. He shaved tobacco from a plug, crammed the bowl of his short, black pipe, picked up a small red coal from the fire with his fingers and laid it on the tobacco. Then he fell back against a great piece of driftwood and sighed with contentment.

"How far have we made, Louis?" the priest asked.

Louis considered, looking out upon the water and down the shoreline, finally scrutinizing the sky.

"Let us say three pipes, mon Père."

Father Baraga decided that this meant about twenty miles and confirmed the estimate in his own mind.

Through what remained of the afternoon Gaudin paddled steadily; the light wind was against them and no use could be made of the small piece of sailcloth that the voyageur had folded in his pack. There was little talk between them, Father Baraga employing the hours with breviary and meditation and Gaudin given over to the monotonous toil of the paddle. He held close to the shore. Twice they met canoes of Indians headed for La Pointe. Each time the Indians changed their courses slightly to bring them close to the missionary's canoe. Brief greetings were exchanged but Gaudin did not stop. He was very abrupt of manner with the second party they met. Out of ear-shot, he explained.

"Pillagers!" he spat contemptuously into the water. "They are from Leech Lake. Bad!"

They kept steadily on their course until some time after the sun had set, Gaudin watching the shore for a particular camping place he knew. Just at dusk they landed and another meal was prepared. Even before the inevitable pipe was smoked out, Gaudin was dozing in the warmth of the fire. By the time it was fully dark they were rolled in their blankets and the voyageur's heavy breathing told Father Baraga that he slept soundly.

The journey was resumed at dawn; they were on the way within a short time after they had emerged from their blankets. Late the next day they entered the mouth of the St. Louis River. Once off the lake, they had a strong, steady current to ascend.

Fond du Lac proved to be a small Indian village gathered about a fur-trading post. It was directly upon the bank of the river, with high wooded hills behind it. The stream was swift here, and Gaudin told the priest that a short distance above was the Grand Portage, circumventing a series of impassable rapids.

They tied the canoe to a stake in the river bank and landed. News of their coming had passed through the village and many Indians appeared suddenly, gathering in a crowd that blocked their path. Almost at once there came bursting through the idle, curious group a huge Canadian shouting his welcome. Father Baraga was quite swept off his feet by the reception of his self-appointed host.

"Ah, mon Père, you are come! *Mon Dieu*, it is good to see you! Come! Come this way! *Allez-vous-en!*" he roared at the close-packed Indians who, apparently accustomed to the vehemence of the trader's enthusiasms, gave way only slightly as he started for the village.

Father Baraga, in the vortex of the throng, was forced to smile. *"Allons,"* he told his one-man reception committee.

Led by the big trader, and with Louis Gaudin close behind him, the priest made his way slowly along the narrow path from the river bank. The excitement of the trader knew no bounds. He shouted incessantly, kicking to right and left at the half-starved dogs that impeded his triumphal march. His words in three languages flew back and forth depending on the direction in which he bellowed.

Into the trading post they marched. Immediately the excited host drove a half-dozen loitering Indians outside. "Get out! Get out! Do you not see that the priest comes to visit Pierre Cotte? Begone! Get outside!" Father Baraga noticed that they showed no ill will as he shoved them out and slammed the door behind them.

The room, dark and ill-smelling, was in great disorder. Father Baraga remained standing in the one spot where his feet had found a cleared space. But he was soon to discover that there was a foundation for Pierre Cotte's enthusiasm. Somewhere in his travels he had acquired a copy of the missionary's Chippewa prayerbook, which contained several hymns. This book he now produced from some hidden recess invisible to his guest. Obviously he felt that he already knew the author of the hymnal.

Suddenly in the middle of an arm-waving, boisterous demonstration of his own conception of proper hymn-singing, it occurred to him that his guest was still standing uncomfortably in the center of the room. He stopped suddenly, his mouth wide open. Then, as suddenly, his solicitude for the priest's comfort became a magnificent physical and oral tirade against all loafers and a series of bellowed directions to unseen menials, punctuated by loud personal apologies to his guest. In this deluge, Father Baraga was seated and served his dinner.

But that evening Pierre Cotte produced his choir!

Ever since he had first brought the little book home to Fond du Lac, he had regularly assembled a few chosen Indians and taught them to sing the hymns by rote. Now the storeroom was filled almost to the point of suffocation with these singers. Pierre, leading them in a lusty voice, required encore after encore of the few hymns the little book contained.

It was a welcome that warmed Father Baraga's heart. He had seen — and where he had least expected it — his book being put to the practical use of which he had dreamed while he was compiling it. How could he have known that a copy would precede him to this far western end of Lake Superior?

During the next few days he preached to the Indians. Many were immediately receptive, thanks to Pierre Cotte. The missionary baptized several. When he suggested that it was an opportune time for visiting the Indians at Leech Lake, Pierre virtually forbade it, rolling his eyes and looking very mysterious. The trader wanted Father Baraga to remain at Fond du Lac indefinitely, but now Louis Gaudin began to hint that it might be wise to return as quickly as possible to La Pointe.

On a raw and disagreeable day priest and voyageur floated down the St. Louis to return home. Several canoes accompanied them part of the way and Father Baraga was forced to promise over and over again that he would return to Fond du Lac as soon as he could.

On Lake Superior the wind was in the west and Gaudin rigged his bit of sail. They moved steadily, the breeze held, the sky cleared, so they decided to travel all night under the stars. For a long time after darkness fell, their way was lit by the eerie luminosity of the Northern Lights — wraith banners streaming far toward the zenith with vivid swiftness and then quickly falling back as though the force that sent them soaring had utterly spent itself. The air was a sharp chillness and Father Baraga wrapped a blanket about his shoulders.

Behind him in the canoe, Louis Gaudin was humming an air — *"Le bon vin m'endort...."*

Father Baraga was conscious of a deep peace. How small we are, he thought, in this vastness, how little we can see and how poorly we understand even that little! In this life surely we are children, capable of knowledge only through love. There are times, he mused, watching the lifting and soaring wraiths of the great lights in the sky, there are times when each human soul lifts and soars out of itself, reaching and aspiring toward the Great Goodness. How quickly these flowing lights subside and fade! Ah yes, something within us pulls us back. Well, but we did soar!

Louis sang softly: " *'L'amour me reveille....'*

"But forgive me, mon Père. I sing but to sing! The night is so beautiful!"

"Sing on, my Louis. We journey beneath the stars but we behold them!"

CHAPTER VII

FATHER BARAGA was made constantly aware of the advancing season. Even before he had gone to Fond du Lac, there had been something portentous in the knowledge that the "John Jacob Astor" had made her last voyage of the year. For several weeks the herring fishery had been unusually active and the small fishing boats of La Pointe returned day after day to deliver their silvery cargoes. Each day, too, traders departed on long journeys to the interior, their canoes heavy with trade goods. More and more of the cedar-bark lodges of the Indians were pulled down or abandoned, and at times there would be flotillas of departing canoes in sight on the lake.

Sometimes great, soft flakes of snow sifted down gently out of a low gray sky. Again, a tiny-particled mist clung and dripped in a world veiled with moisture. Sometimes a sharp, eager wind dashed suddenly out of the northwest — a keen wolf in a flock of mackerel clouds. Then the odor of swirling wood smoke filled all the air and the lake waters danced in brief interludes of too bright sunshine.

But also, for a space, there descended upon the little island world a short season of ineffable peace among the elements. Then one walked about in a warmth of subdued light, in a dream atmosphere. All else was walled off by the pearly haze on the horizon, that shut them within an enchanted quietude where the sun was theirs alone and its long, slanting rays warmed them with a benign warmth like gentle humility.

In this Indian summer Father Baraga often walked alone, following the long, sandy beaches. Watching the lazy waves break slowly, he felt a serene well-being. Only the faint noises that came to him from the settlement — the shrill laughter of children, the quick bark of a dog — kept him related to the little temporal world he knew.

This is a strange and fascinating country, he thought. So serene now, yet soon to be bitter and cruel. Those child voices are happy, yet I know that I shall have to bear hearing them raised in anguish. These people need so little, are content with so little. Soon, when the Angelus sounds, they will pause and make the Sign. And I am beguiled into walking here in the quiet peace of God. Yet well I know that this is only the interlude. For a thousand miles, this vast inland sea touches lands inhabited by the thin remnants of a scattered and hopeless people. I must find them!

Under the black cassock the slight body tensed. The feet in their brown moccasins moved more quickly. His mission was upon him with impelling force. He was walking very rapidly now. His eyes were far off upon the lake and of his immediate surroundings he heard and felt nothing. Then suddenly he stood stock-still. *"Domine,* a contrite and humble heart Thou wilt not despise," he murmured.

After a time he turned purposefully from the shore. The trail led inland through white birches interspersed with small, trim spruce. His pace was quick with nervous energy but his feet were sure and careful on the twisting path.

Through the small windows, the graying twilight of the soft autumn day gave a light that enlarged and distorted, with the feeble help of the tapers, all the interior of the church. The short aisle between the rough wooden pews seemed to stretch away and become the aisle of an ancient and half-remembered cathedral. The hewn timbers of the ceiling lifted, in the murk, to become great, graceful lines forming the arches and groins of some splendid architecture. He was aware of kneeling figures in dim and sanctified semishadow before him. They seemed to be far away and yet very near, so near that he thought he might lay his hand upon each bowed head. As he turned to the sanctuary, the simple, crude altar with its poor furnishings became rich and adorned in the strange light. Murmured phrases of the familiar prayers floated and drifted up to him like echoes in a vaulted apse, redolent with incense. His own and his people's poverty was forgotten. Priest and people were exalted in that little wilderness church.

Father Baraga realized that he loved this wilderness beyond any human explanation. No sequence of thoughts that is the logic of finite minds had been any part of it. He merely saw the ineffable autumn night flung about him and his flock like the mantle of God. A thousand details flooded upon his mind in a full current of affection — long stretches of clean sand leading up to sheer rock cliffs where the waters broke and cascaded, timbered league on league laced by countless limpid streams, frozen white fastnesses with little fir trees green and symmetrical against the snow. In the time that followed, this lifting experience was to recur again and again, even in the depths of loneliness and desolation.

At last winter came and the little community was beleaguered. Now the missionary devoted himself very largely to sedentary duties. Because his zeal called for compensating physical action, these duties were often irksome. Writing and teaching occupied much of his time. The attendance at his daily school was fairly regular once winter made indoor life more tolerable for these children who lived so close to nature.

Religious instruction for those who wintered at La Pointe could now be systematic and thorough. The altar boys were carefully trained and the Church's rites moved in smooth, sure ceremony. A choir was organized and given regular rehearsals. Theophile Remillard had a fine singing voice and he was assisted by the brothers Antoine and Jean Baptiste Gaudin. A choir loft was installed, though a short ladder did duty for stairs. The stations were erected — plain, neat crosses built in the carpenter shop by old Antoine Perrinier. Father Baraga sometimes went to the shop to help the carpenter, enjoying the release of physical activity, and feeling too something of the artist's satisfaction in the contact of sharp tools with soft, dry wood. Perrinier was adept at wood sculpture and took great pride in embellishing the altar.

The missionary also found time to complete several writing tasks. He believed that European readers, especially those who contributed to his mission, desired accurate information about the life of the American Indians. But the compositions on which he worked with most enjoyment were those in the Chippewa language: a prayerbook and a life of Christ. The preparation of these works challenged him and often he puzzled for hours, writing and rewriting in order to convey just the thought he desired, in words that the Indians would most easily comprehend.

But often he fretted under the restraint that winter put upon his activities. Twice he made snowshoe trips to the mainland to visit a few Indians wintering not far in the interior. These were not long trips, but they served to release him from a feeling of idleness. He was abstemious and self-critical. Once,

when he was taking his meals for a time at the home of Seraphin
Lacomb, Madame Lacomb offered apologies for the single dish
she could provide. It was hulled corn. Unable to understand
the need for her apologies, he abruptly left the table and fled
from the house. He accused himself bitterly of having given
the impression that he desired better food or that he cared in
any way about the food that was provided. Gradually he came
to realize, however, that the poor woman might entirely mis-
understand his action. Returning to find her in tears, he explained in simple and honest words why he had left. His kindness and humility reassured her, but Father Baraga was heart-
broken that his lack of self-control had caused the good woman
embarrassment and grief.

The season wore on, its dreadful monotony sometimes becoming akin to actual physical pain. Storm on the heels of
storm drove across the wide expanse of Lake Superior to lash
the little settlement at La Pointe.

In such a tempest there came to him one day through a child
in his school the information that an old squaw, Goose, was
very sick and wanted the priest. Her relatives, when they had
departed for their winter hunting grounds, had believed it
better for her, in her feeble state, to remain at La Pointe. Father
Baraga had visited her often and she had told him shyly of the
glorious days of her maidenhood when she had been considered
beautiful. Then she had been called, she said, Water Flower.
Yet for all her willingness to talk to him, she had continued
firm against the acceptance of his teaching.

When he understood that the child had actually brought
him a message, he left the children in charge of young Vincent
Roy, the oldest boy in the class, hurriedly fastened his snow-

He prayed, holding the cold, withered, twisted hand.

[67]

shoes and started for the sick woman's lodge. The cold was unmerciful. The air was so thick with blown snow that he could scarcely see his hand before his face. The sharp, driven pellets almost blinded him. He lost the trail again and again, finding it only by the feel of his snowshoes on the harder surface beneath the new snow.

But at last he came to the old woman's lodge. The snow was drifted before the entrance so that he had to unlash a snowshoe to shovel it aside. On his hands and knees he crawled through the low passageway. Inside the hut it was cold and dark, and the air was fetid with the smell of sickness. Shivering violently and panting from the effort of his swift race, he was compelled to remain a long moment in his kneeling posture, for he was quite spent.

At last, a low groan guiding him, he crawled over to where she was huddled in old, stiff blankets. He searched and found a thin, gnarled hand, cold as his own. He put his ear close to her face and heard her whisper in breaths that flickered, then halted.

Rising, he kindled a light, found the water bucket, broke the icy sheet that covered the water and filled the drinking gourd.

"I baptize thee in the name of the Father and of the Son and of the Holy Ghost."

For a long while after she died he prayed there, holding the cold, withered, twisted hand. He thought of her shy pride the day she had told him of her youth. He thought of the myriad hard tasks the gnarled hand had performed in the cruel economy of a bitter country. He laid the hand gently on her breast.

"*Ave Maria....*"

Outside, he fastened the cover of the entrance carefully and heaped snow against it to hold it tight.

CHAPTER VIII

SPRING came in, that year of 1836, with feet of lead. Its tardiness was even more grievous to the little settlement than the cold had been. Winter had retreated a short way but spring did not take up the relinquished ground, and in the interim the weather was unusually oppressive. Patience became frayed. Travel was dangerous, for snow and ice were unsafe. The Crust Moon, when warm, sunny days melt the top snow which freezes at night, appeared not at all that year. The old men and women, born in the Lake Superior country, agreed that it was the worst winter and spring they had ever known. The missionary's exasperation at his enforced idleness was almost at the breaking point.

Spring did come at last. It was niggardly of its warmth and charm; only occasionally the sun broke through a low-arched, sodden sky. Yet one day the foliage on the white birches appeared like a thin, green mist. Slothful and miserly, spring had come to La Pointe.

During the winter Father Baraga had sat beside the fires of his parishioners and talked with them of many things. He absorbed all that they told him about the Lake Superior country. The Indian settlement on the Ontonagon River interested him increasingly, and he had resolved to go there as early as conditions permitted.

Antoine Perrinier, laying aside his work in the shop and lighting his pipe, told him: "Yes, that is so, mon Père. It is 'the place of the bowl.' My mother told me how the river got its name. Many, many years ago a young girl dropped her wooden bowl in the river and it floated away. She ran along the bank

and cried, *'On-to-nagon, on-to-nagon!'* That is what it means —
'I have lost my bowl!' My mother told me the story when I was
a small boy. She was a Chippewa woman."

Mr. Oakes, the assistant factor, idle in the Company store,
added information: "The place has always been occupied by
a band of Indians. They acknowledge Buffalo as chief but they
have a subchief named Kon-te-ka — 'Buoy.' They are really
part of the La Pointe band. They are great fishermen, and they
stay at Ontonagon because there is good fishing ground near
the mouth of the river. I think some of them are the best canoe-
men on Lake Superior."

"Now, about that copper rock in the Ontonagon River, mon
Père," old Perrinier said one day. "I have never seen it, but it
is there. Yes, it is solid copper! Several Indians who have seen
it have told me about it. It is very large and it sticks up out of
the water. Kon-te-ka told me a long time ago that, when he
was a boy, Englishmen came and tried to make a mine there, but
some of them were killed and the rest went away."

"The Indians do not like to talk about that copper rock,"
Mr. Oakes related further. "I myself have never seen it. It is
quite a distance up the river, I am told. Oh yes, I am certain
that such a copper rock exists. For my part, I say let it stay
there!"

Dr. Borup, too, had something to offer: "When I first came
to Lake Superior, I talked with Henry Schoolcraft at Sault Ste.
Marie. You know, he is the Indian agent who married one of
John Johnston's daughters. She's a granddaughter of Waub-o-
jeeg — 'White Fisher' — the greatest chief the Chippewas ever
had. He lived here at La Pointe. Schoolcraft is a very studious
man and his Indian connections permit him to acquire very
accurate information. When I talked with him, he had just been

on the Ontonagon and had seen the copper rock. He said it was a considerable distance up the river. The Indian village is at the mouth of the river, you understand. As I recall, School-craft told me he had examined the rock very carefully and thought there might be a ton or more of solid copper in it. I think he said it lay a little in the water. It had been hacked and chopped and there were broken tools near by on the bank of the river. It is certain that pieces of copper had been cut off and carried away. Now, that was quite a few years ago and the rock is still there, and I think it will go right on being there for quite a few years to come. What good is it? How could you get a thing like that out of the country? The river is not navigable all the way even for canoes; it would be necessary to portage over a range or two of great hills. Besides, I think the Indians would make trouble for anyone who tried to take that copper rock away. I have heard that they put tobacco on it for Gitche Manitou."*

Father Baraga made no comment, but he thought: I am not so sure. I have seen these restless Americans at the ports on the lower lakes. Let them learn for certain that there is copper on Lake Superior and they will penetrate every corner of this wilderness to find it. And when that day comes, woe to these poor Indians!

So one day while there was still enough ice on the bays to make travel possible, the missionary set out on foot for the mouth of the Ontonagon. His companion was Basil Cadotte. Their route took them directly eastward. The distance was too great to be traversed in one sun, and it was their plan to travel a long day, putting ashore at nightfall to camp.

---

*One of the variants of the Indian name for the Supreme Being.

In order to make speed they kept well out from land, since the winter storms had piled the ice in great, impassable ridges along the shore. The leg of the journey that would take them back to land at nightfall was lost motion but the circumstances required it. The trip was not at all an uncommon one; many at La Pointe had made it at one time or another. No one counseled against it now.

The travelers started at dawn and pushed rapidly on for several hours. They watched for the easiest passages ahead and talked little. The day was well along but the murky weather imposed a close horizon. They had seen no landmark since leaving La Pointe. It had been understood that as the day wore on, they would pick up the Porcupine Mountains a little to their right and set their course by these: they would make shore while the Porcupines were still visible, and keep that great landmark always on their right hand. That was the counsel and that was the plan.

We cannot know how far from land they were when they discovered their danger.

Suddenly they saw open water before them. For an hour or more the wind had been steadily rising out of the southeast. Basil, slightly ahead, turned and started running as fast as he could in the direction from which they had come, calling frantically to Father Baraga to follow him. But before the priest could make any response, Basil pulled up short on the very edge of what they now realized was a detached piece of ice.

Cadotte was in a panic. He rushed here and there trying to find a way back. Finally he came toward Father Baraga, gasping for breath, pale and trembling.

"We are lost, mon Père!"

His face was terrible to behold. His eyes stared wide and wild. Suddenly he dropped on his knees before the priest and started to pray. Choking sobs interrupted the wildly racing words.

Father Baraga laid a hand on Basil's bowed head and surveyed the situation. He was undisturbed except that he felt a wrench of pity for his companion. It was plain that they were in a field of broken ice, and he realized that the piece on which they were temporarily safe might split at any moment. The wind was strong; they must be drifting rapidly with the field. There was absolutely nothing that they could do to help themselves.

"Calm yourself, my Basil," he said gently, his hand still resting firmly on the head of the kneeling man. "Let us be patient and await the will of God."

Basil scrambled to his feet. "But see, mon Père, we are surely lost! We are out in the open lake!"

"Perhaps we are not lost. That is not for us to say now, my son. That is only for God to know. Perhaps we drift even now toward land."

"No, no, mon Père! You are a stranger — you do not understand. We are surely lost! If we drift toward the land the ice will pile up on the shore and we will be killed. If we drift out to sea we will starve or freeze. Oh, we are lost! Pray for us, Père Baraga!"

"Come, my Basil." The missionary reached out and took Basil's shaking hand. "Pick up your cap because the wind is very cold. So. Now we shall wait quietly and see what God wills for us. He knows we are here. Let us sing a hymn and be patient."

Still holding Basil's hand in his own, Father Baraga led him about on the ice. He thought the man frantic enough to do some foolish act, so he did not loosen his grasp. While they walked the priest raised his voice in song. Basil attempted to join in the hymn now and then, snatching at tune and words in a kind of dumb desperation. Gradually, as his companion went on from hymn to hymn, he became calmer and at last seemed quite resigned. Father Baraga kept moving, kept singing. Warm as they had been from the fast pace of the journey, to sit or stand now in the bitter wind would have been fatal. To sing lustily was a kind of physical exercise in itself, and it served the further purpose of trading exaltation for hopelessness, trust in God for despair. Above all, it was efficacious prayer.

They walked and sang for a long time. The hours passed and the priest knew that night was now close.

Suddenly Basil cried out in the middle of a song.

"Land, mon Père!"

Majestically their great block of ice was floating shoreward with easy and steady movement. They saw the intervening waters slowly diminish. It was as though other great floating blocks around them maneuvered to let them pass. They stood close together and neither spoke. Basil's face registered his fear, his expectation, his hope, in rapidly changing expressions. He lived a lifetime in that last mile. Deliberately they approached the low shore of a wide bay. And the Porcupine Mountains loomed gigantic on their right hand.

Finally Father Baraga spoke.

"See, my Basil, we shall camp here. It would have taken us many hours of weary walking to have reached this place. Now we are here quickly and with no effort. But we shall have to get wet, do you observe? Yes, we have a complete wetting to endure, and it is very cold. But we are safe!"

[74]

Their great block of ice was floating steadily shoreward.

[75]

Safe they were — and wet and miserable. Their garments froze before they could start a fire. They managed a shelter on the shore of Union Bay, cooked a meal and spent the night as best they could. At daylight they lashed their snowshoes on and late that afternoon the priest and his companion were welcomed by the Indians on the Ontonagon.

CHAPTER IX

AS THE belated season advanced slowly toward summer, La Pointe became again a populous and animated scene. Out of the far interior where they had wintered came the Company's traders, their large canoes heavily laden with packs of furs. The air about the fort was full of the meaty, musky odors of the raw skins, which were now unpacked to be cleaned, dried and sorted, and then arranged in the packing frames for shipment on the "John Jacob Astor." Everyone was busy and the place was gay with life.

Indian families were returning daily, many bringing their winter's take of fur directly to the fort. Maple sugar in mocucks of birch bark was part of the cargo of every Indian canoe. The cedar-bark lodges were put up quickly and their number grew day by day.

It was late in May when Father Baraga, busy with his increased duties as the island people returned, found opportunity to keep his promise of going back to Fond du Lac. Several large freighting canoes were leaving La Pointe to pick up the furs collected at the trading post there. They were well manned for this was to be a quick trip in line of commerce. Mr. Agnew, who was in charge, had the duty of checking and listing the furs at Fond du Lac before bringing them in.

Out on the lake and beyond the shelter of the Apostle Islands they headed westerly against a stiff breeze. The men worked in rhythm and the canoes went steadily on hour after hour. A good voice sang:

> "Home, we are leaving thee!
> Cheerful let our hearts be,
> Supported by hope!"

Then all the men joined in the chorus:

> "Away, then, away!
> Away, then, away!"

"Ah, mon Père," Louis Gaudin laughed, "this is like the *canot du gouverneur! * Only it is the *canot du Père!* "

All the men in the canoe laughed too. Father Baraga had heard of the famous *canot du gouverneur*. It was the magnificent canoe in which the manager of one of the old fur companies made quick trips of inspection from Montreal, entering Lake Superior at Sault Ste. Marie. With a crew of picked voyageurs, it was a fast canoe indeed. All these songs that the men now sang had come off the St. Lawrence River, part and parcel of the traditions of the fur trade. What legends these men and their fathers have built — what incredible tales they tell, the priest thought. Now they were voyageurs in the *canot du Père!* It amused him as it had amused the men, and he knew they were happy to have him with them.

[77]

They were astonished to encounter stray pieces of ice in the lake — and here it was the Moon of Flowers! That brought up tales of the hardships of the past winter, tales of incredible suffering, but which he could not well doubt. In a matter-of-fact way each man related some specific experience as if it were merely a piece of news. Father Baraga thought there were no limits to their hardihood and courage.

But now, following the line of these narrations, he heard references to his own experience with Basil Cadotte in the field of broken ice off the Ontonagon, and he realized with astonishment that they believed a miracle had taken place, and very much wanted to hear his own description of the journey. Basil has been telling some vastly embellished tale, he thought. He was content that his adventure on the ice had made him acceptable in a new way with these men, but he would say no word of it.

At Fond du Lac he decided not to return with the fur canoes both because they were leaving so soon and because they were heavily laden. Pierre Cotte, voluble and excited, was kept busy with the transfer of the skins at his post, but he found time to urge that Father Baraga remain, promising to provide means of transportation to La Pointe later. So for two weeks the missionary devoted his time to the Indians at Fond du Lac; before he left, he baptized fourteen adults and several children.

It was June when he made the return trip to La Pointe in the company of two old Indians, both of whom he had converted. Their progress was very slow. Even when the weather was favorable, his companions seemed to care little about time. Sudden squalls, with terrific flashes of lightning and tremendous thunderclaps, drove them ashore several times. Torrents of rain fell, followed by hours of muggy heat when the air seemed to press upon the body and mosquitoes and small black flies became a very real torment. Father Baraga's face and hands were bitten and swollen, his garments sodden. Even after the rains ceased they could not take to the lake at once as the water remained high and dangerous for hours. The last day of the trip they had no food at all.

But they reached La Pointe at last and the missionary set about his work more energetically than ever. He baptized twenty-eight in the days immediately following his return. While he was gone the "John Jacob Astor" had arrived with a large packing case addressed to him, which the factor had had delivered to his house. Father Baraga saw at once that it had been sent by the Leopoldine Society in Vienna. He opened it quickly. It contained the articles he had so long needed: scores of rosaries, large and small medals, quantities of colored holy cards, and scapulars that he knew had been embroidered in many a religious house in his native country, the makers meanwhile praying for him in his faraway mission.

If the winter had been especially dreadful in a country where all winters are terrible, the summer proved to be ideal in both the kindness of the weather and the progress of Father Baraga's work. The Indians knew him now; they received his visits with pleasure and listened to his words with understanding. His sincerity when he spoke of their poverty and his own; his generosity in giving such things as he had to give and his simple acceptance of their hospitality; his willingness to undergo without complaint every hardship to be with them — all these things made access to them easy and contact effective.

Serenity came also to his own spirit. In the long summer evenings the idyllic scene revolved about him. He knew the woodcutting hour, when the young Indian maidens went into the woods to procure faggots for the domestic fires. There followed them unobserved the young men who were their suitors, and in the peaceful twilight the attentive ear heard the murmur of their voices and the lilt of quick, happy laughter in the fringe of woodland. Old men sat smoking and dreaming of their own young loves and the exploits of their youth. Women minded their babies and children played their games in the fading light, the unconscious urge to excel strong within them. On all these things, Father Baraga thought, a gentle benediction descended.

CHAPTER X

IN THE talk that he heard all about him, an ever-recurring subject was the prospective removal of the Indians westward by the government. Dr. Borup informed him that when the last payment had been held at La Pointe, the Indian agent himself had given impetus to the rumor.

"He didn't exactly say that it was certain to be done," the factor admitted. "He didn't say he had orders to carry out, but he did say he thought the order was not far off."

Father Baraga found the Indians deeply disturbed over the matter. In their resentment they vowed that they would not go westward at the government's order, but would go instead to the north shore of Lake Superior, where they would live under the English flag. But their general depression and their sad and wistful words reflected their helplessness. He sensed that they would not cross the lake to find new homes. He felt sure that, when the order came, they would move westward with heavy hearts.

Anticipating that time, he resolved to go in the autumn and acquaint himself with the country west of the lake, that was apparently to be the future home of his Indians. Perhaps he might make the migration easier for them when it came. Perhaps he might help, if he were foresighted now, to ease the friction between those Indians living about Leech and Sandy Lakes and these Lake Superior Indians who would be forced to settle among them.

He did not have to wait long to put his resolution into effect. Soon, he learned, a fleet of trading canoes would leave La Pointe to establish posts in the interior. Their schedule would not give him the time he needed to look over the country west of the lake thoroughly, but he would do the best he could.

The plan fixed in his mind, he applied himself with his usual diligence to immediate duties. Already the seasonal unrest was on the Indians. Soon they would begin to depart for the winter's hunting. But a spell of pleasant weather beguiled the island settlement for a while, and in the midst of it the expedition was launched. The route lay by Fond du Lac, so the first leg of the journey was not new to him.

In conversations with them before he departed Father Baraga perceived that the factor and his assistant felt it necessary to give him advice. They told him, in detail and with considerable emphasis, about the bad reputation of the Sandy Lake Indians, a renegade band of the Chippewas. He already knew something of them. His La Pointe and Fond du Lac Indians had a distrustful fear of the Indians west of Lake Superior. In a way, this attitude was more marked than their attitude toward their blood enemies, the Sioux. The Sioux they respected as proper enemies. But for these others — this outcast band of their own nation — they had a mute but definite abhorrence. "The Pillagers," they called them, and when he inquired about them, his Indians answered reluctantly, evasively.

"Father Baraga," Dr. Borup said, "you have traveled in many places and for several years among the Indians. I notice that you have learned that it is often wisest to leave the young men alone, even here at La Pointe. In our business we have learned many things too. It is often our practice to treat some of the young men with outright coldness, allowing not even the smallest degree of familiarity. Once your guard is down, many of these young men become insolent and overbearing. They are very haughty and I have had more than one experience to teach me that they are revengeful. At times like the present, when the Indians are excited about the talk that the government will move them, only the wise counsel of men like Buffalo restrains the young men from open resentment, which would mean bloodshed.

"But," the factor continued, "you have as yet had no experience with the Pillagers. If you propose to go among them, I feel that you should be given a very explicit warning. I sum it up by saying that we here at the fort will not do business with them."

"Judging by the name they bear, I assume you mean they steal and plunder. Is it that they would steal your trade goods?" the priest inquired.

"That — and more. They do not hesitate to murder. There is not a trader or an Indian on Lake Superior who is not secretly afraid of them. They are not warriors, you understand. They are not brave. They are thieves and murderers."

"And worse," added Mr. Oakes. "They are cannibals!"

"God forbid!" Father Baraga cried.

"You have no idea of their filth and greed and heathenish practices," Oakes went on. "Their poverty exceeds anything you have ever known, I am sure. Their laziness is beyond comprehension. And they pride themselves on these things!"

"But I understand that they live directly on one of your most important trade routes, and that you bring trade goods in and furs out through their territory," the priest observed.

"Oh, yes," Dr. Borup replied. "I venture to say that our post at Sandy Lake, over all the years it has been there, has held many thousands of dollars' worth of fur. That route is one of the most famous fur trails in the northwest. It was used by the older companies before our time. But it has cost something! It has cost a pretty large price, I am afraid."

"Just who are these Pillagers?" asked the missionary.

"Well, sir, I believe they are a renegade mixture. They are not numerous and there has probably been a great deal of intermarrying. They appear to be a colony of criminal Indians. We are telling you these things so that you may be prepared. We insist that you do not stay alone with these devils under any circumstances — not even for an hour. Indeed, our permission to go with the expedition must be based on your promise to be careful."

"But I am not afraid."

"You are too fearless, Father Baraga," Oakes exclaimed.

"We know your indifference to danger, but this is another matter. If anything should happen to you it would have a very bad effect all up and down the lake. We would be blamed."

"I promise," Father Baraga said. "Perhaps if I am especially careful now, I can win the confidence of these Indians at a later time. Yes, I will be careful. I give you my word."

Favorable weather held. After a brief stop at Fond du Lac they continued up the St. Louis for three miles to their first portage. Called the Grand Portage, it extended for nine miles. Here Father Baraga beheld for the first time on a large scale the superb strength and endurance of Lake Superior voyageurs.

Packs weighing some hundred and fifty pounds were quickly made from the goods in the canoes. As fast as these packs were made ready, the voyageurs lifted them and adjusted them on their backs. While the burden rested just below the curve of the bearer's neck, it was not borne entirely by his shoulders. To each pack was attached a tumpline — a strap fastened about the forehead — so that much of the weight could be supported part of the time by the muscles of his neck. There was no shirking or complaining about the size of the packs. On the contrary, these hardy men took pride in selecting larger ones than the average.

When the canoes were empty, they were turned upside down and shouldered by several men. The voyageurs who carried the canoes did not walk slowly as would be expected of men bearing heavy loads. Instead they ran for a short distance, rested a brief interval, and then ran again. Father Baraga could see the wisdom of this procedure. The important thing was to get over the ground and be rid of the galling weight as quickly as possible.

The priest insisted on attempting to carry a pack, and at last the men laughingly adjusted one on his back. He made no effort to maintain the quick pace of the others on the trail, but even so, the weight and the poor footing soon exhausted him. Toward the end of the portage he sat down to rest more and more frequently, and those who passed him begged him to relinquish his load to them. These offers he refused. He was determined to take the pack the full distance. Finally he stumbled and fell prone beneath it. He smiled ruefully, glad that no one had witnessed his accident. But even while he was congratulating himself he felt the weight lifted. Big Alexis pulled the harness off him with a gentle tug, laughing at his protest. He had not heard the Canadian's feet on the trail behind him.

The huge voyageur tossed Father Baraga's pack atop his own and swung into the half-trotting pace of the packers. He was soon out of sight. It was an enormous relief to the priest's aching muscles, and he was compelled to admit to himself that undoubtedly he was "too much sweat" — the voyageur term for "tired." Alexis had said, "Too much sweat, mon Père! I tak' heem easy!"

After the Grand Portage, the canoes were not long in the water before Knife Portage was reached. Its name came from the fact that the tilted thin strata in the exposed ridge had weathered for a considerable distance to sharp edges. Father Baraga was glad he had no pack to bear over that difficult trail. Thus the expedition progressed for some days, with carry after carry and short river journeys in between. Each night they camped only from darkness to dawn. The men were always cheerful, and they made it evident that they were pleased to have Father Baraga with them. At last they entered the smaller East Savan River and their course was westerly. There was trouble in swamps now and sometimes they were in mud and water to their waists.

When they finally arrived at the village of the Pillagers, the missionary felt that all the factor and his assistant had told him must be true. He was shocked at the poverty and open depravity he beheld. The Indians' indifference to his words saddened him. And he was distressed at the shortness of the time. Interior traders met the expedition here, took their supplies and departed at once. His own party was already making quick preparations for the return trip to La Pointe.

Not long before his departure, Father Baraga stood talking to an aged Indian and his squaw. A young Indian, indescribably filthy and almost naked, his face painted in hideous designs, walked past the little group and deliberately jostled the priest until he lost his balance and fell. Ignoring the insult, Father Baraga rose and continued his conversation with the two old people.

Alexis sauntered up presently and advised him that they were almost ready to start. As the priest was saying a last word to the couple, he saw the young Indian again approaching, now openly insolent. Coming close, he spat in Father Baraga's face, uttered a demoniacal shriek and danced away. Before the missionary recovered from his surprise, Alexis had sprung forward and with one blow of his fist knocked the young Indian kicking. Then the big trader was standing over his victim with his belt knife drawn.

Father Baraga rushed to seize Alexis' wrist, pushing him away with all his strength.

"No, no, Alexis!" he cried. "God forbid!"

The big man with the Indian sprawled between his feet was white with rage. Perhaps no other power on earth could have stayed his hand at that moment. He could have brushed the slight priest aside in an instant, but he stood perfectly still. Slowly his great, tense body relaxed. Father Baraga's hand rested on his arm. Together they walked off.

A little way and Alexis stopped.

"But why, mon Père?" he asked, his intent gaze on the priest.

"O my Alexis! We must forgive him — he does not know any better."

Alexis looked doubtfully at him.

"Yes, and he is our brother," Father Baraga added. Alexis looked still more doubtful.

They walked in silence to the canoes.

CHAPTER XI

THE summer of 1838 brought Father Baraga new and varied problems. The Chippewas renewed their warfare with the Sioux. While only the young men were engaged, there was a marked restlessness among all the Indians on Lake Superior.

That summer, too, his sister Antonia came to La Pointe to help him.

Then, late in the season, more than three thousand Indians assembled there for the annual government payment.

Finally, his little church received its first visit from the Bishop, who came to dedicate it. Anticipating this happy solemnity, Father Baraga built an addition to the church and joined his own house to it in the one building operation.

The spectacle of the Indian payment was not new to the missionary for he had attended other payments at Mackinac Island and on the Grand River. At La Pointe this year it was held in August. For many days the Indians had been arriving; some of them, he learned, had come a thousand miles. He knew only a small number among the growing throng, and welcomed the opportunity to study the others and extend his acquaintance with them. But he was saddened to discover that the Indians of the interior were even poorer than those on Lake Superior, and that their general attitude was one either of open unfriendliness or of beggarly servility, both equally offensive.

Three thousand Indians at La Pointe made a sizable camp, and there was no order about the encampment. It was summer and for most of them the sojourn was to be brief. The lodges they set up were mere makeshifts, temporary shelters from sun and rain. Some families did not trouble to provide even these but were content to call the little space about an open fire their domicile, sleeping anywhere at night.

It was a rule of the government, strictly enforced, that no Indian, whether man, woman or child, could receive payment except in his own hand. If the individual was not present in person, his name was passed over on the payment list. Consequently every eligible Indian had come, from the helpless aged to the papoose on its mother's back. In addition, every Indian seemed to have brought along his dog for good measure.

The dogs fought continually. The naked children ran about everywhere. The women smoked their pipes and pottered indifferently at domestic tasks. The young men engaged in boisterous games of physical prowess or gambled in silent, tense groups at pagessan, a game somewhat like a combination of dice and chess. The old men sat in idle circles and smoked and droned.

Through Buffalo, Father Baraga arranged to meet all of the chief men of the tribe in council. A great lodge had been erected near the beach and some little distance from the fort. Here many councils were held as well as certain ceremonial proceedings, more or less secret.

When the priest was permitted to enter the council, he spoke briefly and simply of his desire to live among the members of the tribe, traveling to their villages whenever he could. He asked permission to teach their children, and explained the need of all of them to worship God. He made it plain that he was poor in worldly goods, that he had no presents to give them, but that he was anxious to share with them what little he had and willing to suffer with them the hard life they lived. Explaining, however, that he could not hope to find the time and the means to go to each of their far and scattered homes, he invited them to visit him while they were at La Pointe. Finally, he showed them a crucifix and told them its meaning.

Afterward he noted, when he met them about the encampment, that their manner toward him was more friendly and the "boo-zous" they exchanged with him were more cordial. Some of the chiefs, accepting his invitation, came to call upon him at his house and asked to be shown the interior of the church. They were delighted when the bell was rung. In turn they invited him to come to their villages and speak longer to them about God and the Son of God.

When the government agent and his party arrived, the excitement increased. The weather being pleasant, it was decided to use the plaza between the Company stores as the place of payment. Accordingly, tables were set up in this open space and the money and goods made ready for distribution.

The Indian nature loves deliberate ceremony, so the proceedings were slow and leisurely. The agent made a long speech. Many of the chiefs made speeches — all stressing their poverty. No one seemed to be in a hurry; the speech-making took all of one day and part of another.

On the morning of the day set for the actual payment to begin, a tribal dance was held. Most of the men wore only loincloths, their bodies painted with weird patterns, and their faces perfect examples of grotesque art. The colors used were white, black, red and blue; in many cases half the face was painted solidly in one color and the other half in another, and on these backgrounds strange and horrible designs were imposed. The crude drums were beaten in a monotonous rhythm as two or three dancers contorted their bodies in the center of revolving circles of braves. Uncanny yells and screeches were raised in a continuous din.

The dance was stopped at intervals during which individual warriors gave harangues, telling of their personal deeds of valor, cunning and cruelty. Brave after brave spoke, each one exhibiting the scalps he had taken in battle as proof of his prowess.

Father Baraga, watching and listening, was horrified at the bloody recitals. He thought they would never end. But the Indian listeners were spellbound and their "Ho, ho's" were raised in an approving chorus after each dreadful tale.

At last the payment started. It was a regulation of the government, and a ceremony relished by the Indians, that each payee should, on presenting himself at the paying table, touch the agent's quill as his receipt was entered on the list. The chief men were asked to make their marks, holding the pen in their own hands. But as the payment dragged along among the lesser ones, the agent merely struck the quill across each Indian's hand as his name was called off the list and the money handed over.

There sat also at the paying table one of the American Fur Company's representatives, Dr. Borup, Mr. Oakes or Mr. Agnew. Under their hands were the Company's accounts with the individual Indians, and as each came up, whatever he owed was pre-empted immediately. Seldom did any Indian dispute the accuracy of his account even when all of his payment money had to be handed over. In many cases even this did not balance his account with the traders; nevertheless the Indian's hand was struck with the quill and his receipt entered.

The payment money was silver. The payment goods on this occasion were blue cloth and hats and caps. Each Indian had a credit of four dollars and either a small piece of the cloth, a hat or a cap. There was also a limited number of blue coats with brass buttons.

To the missionary it was a grim spectacle. Some of these Indians had made perilous trips of a thousand miles for this pittance and this trash. He did not find it amusing to see them put the brass-buttoned coats on their naked bodies and strut proudly. He found it pitiful. He examined one of the garments and it was cheap and sleazy. Fantastic and outrageous, he thought, and all the more reprehensible because the Indians were so childish. He turned homeward shaken and saddened.

He did not see the gambling that followed the payment. The stakes were mostly the goods that had been distributed, since few Indians had received any money. Nor did he see the *manie au pot* that evening; for, as at all payments of the kind, whiskey had been smuggled into La Pointe for the occasion. But he did hear the drunken shrieks, and shivered to think what they portended.

So was another installment paid on the purchase price of the Indian lands by the United States of America. Those lands

[91]

were yet awaiting the exploitation of their minerals, their timber and their water power.

Antonia arrived at La Pointe soon after the annual payment. Father Baraga was thankful that she had not witnessed it. His own La Pointe Indians had not behaved badly and their conduct was all that saved him from complete discouragement. He was compelled to chide himself, to emphasize over and over again to himself that his mission was not for a day or a year, but that he must be satisfied with any positive results, however meager, after a lifetime of effort and devotion.

None of this, however, to Antonia.

He waited for her at the wharf and greeted her with gentle affection. In all truth, her coming was a little more than he thought he could endure.

Antonia was now a widow. Father Baraga had performed the marriage ceremony that united her with that handsome young Knight of the Holy Roman Empire, Sir Felix de Hoeffern. It was one of the earliest acts of his priesthood, in 1824. He had always remembered the frail beauty of her delicate features uplifted to him, framed in the bridal veil.

His letters to her and to Amalia had been almost frantic in their attempt to dissuade her from joining his mission. At last he told them the truth about the long and terrible Lake Superior winters, which must be spent in dwellings less fit and comfortable than the castle stables; of the coarse and frugal meals served rudely and made palatable only by hunger; of the loneliness, the filth and the dire poverty to be endured. "O my little Antonia," he had cried out in one of his letters, "dear little companion of my childhood, it must not be!"

But Antonia was firm in her decision. When he realized that nothing could deter her, he arranged for her to stop in Baltimore and in Philadelphia for training, and then saw to it that she was placed for a time at Mackinac Island, for life was less harsh in that older community.

Well, Antonia had come now to La Pointe. She could relieve him of much of the work of the school. She had some training for the work she had to do, and at Mackinac she had acquired a little experience in conducting classes.

It was at the beginning of September that Bishop Rese arrived from Detroit. La Pointe was the far outpost of his far-flung diocese. On this visit, he dedicated St. Joseph's Church and confirmed one hundred and twelve converts.

CHAPTER XII

AUTUMN was well advanced when word came to the missionary that Spotted Feather and his band on the north shore wanted him to come to them. Spotted Feather's messenger reported that there was much sickness in the village.

A few minutes after the message was delivered, Louis Gaudin, at work on his boat, looked up to discover the priest beside him. He had no more than greeted his visitor when Father Baraga announced:

"We must start at once!"

Something in his tone, some expression on his face, startled

Louis even more than the words. Father Baraga stood there as though he might be merely on his way from the fort to the church, but the voyageur noticed that he gripped his breviary so tightly that his knuckles were white.

"At once!" he repeated.

"But where, mon Père?"

"To Spotted Feather's village on the north shore!"

If the priest had said "To Montreal," the voyageur would not have been more astonished. He stared in bewilderment, eyes blinking and mouth agape.

Father Baraga stepped toward the boat.

"But, Père Baraga," Gaudin cried, spreading his hands in a wide gesture, "we have no provisions, no blankets, no nothing! Wait, if we must go, let us make ready."

"No, Louis!" The priest's voice was a little sharp. "There is not time for such things. We are as ready as we need be. We start at once!"

They embarked, Louis protesting even while he worked. The missionary remained silent, apparently satisfied as long as the boat moved. Gaudin dipped steadily and talked rapidly.

Well offshore, Father Baraga carefully took his bearings. Then he said quietly:

"Now, straight across, my Louis."

Louis Gaudin could not believe his ears. He stopped paddling the boat altogether.

"Mon Dieu!" he cried. "No one makes that traverse, mon Père!"

"You and I shall make it, Louis."

"Oh no, no! If we must go, let us be sensible, mon Père! We will follow the land like sane voyageurs. That is the only way we will ever arrive. No man makes that traverse!"

"Head straight across," the priest replied firmly. "See, we will have a favorable offshore breeze. It blows from the south and we shall use the piece of sailcloth. We shall go quickly."

Every fiber of the experienced voyageur protested. It was suicidal. Never in all his life had he heard of anyone attempting to cross Lake Superior in a small boat like this. Sixty miles of open water in a frail canoe! Fear and wrath surged through him. And yet —

He hoisted the little spruce spar with its tiny spread of sail, and under the impulse of the strong breeze the canoe leaped forward. He steered north.

Now Louis was as silent as Father Baraga. He set himself, grim and sullen, to his task. The priest was calmly reading his breviary. Soon the land behind them disappeared.

No other lake in the world is as moody as Lake Superior. That reputation has belonged to it since its history was recorded, and to this day is imprinted on the marine advice of the two governments which supervise its navigation. Unusually subject to sudden and disastrous squalls, the mariner is told. Those who sail Superior have seen the wind jump without warning from one quarter to the direct opposite. They have seen crosswinds out of every quarter in a matter of minutes. And they have seen a gale blow suddenly out of calm weather.

Now, Gaudin's fear was allayed only by the boat's speed before a strong and steady south wind. The two men were not uncomfortable in the mild temperature and the water was an undulating restlessness on which they lifted and fell in a long rhythm. Every hope, Gaudin knew, lay in the element of time. Under the extremely favorable conditions of the moment, a few hours would take them across. But he had no confidence whatever in any weather on Lake Superior. A venturesome lifetime had taught him its capriciousness. With tense attention to his navigation, he measured every foot they made.

There was no mistaking the first ominous sign when it came. To a stranger on Lake Superior it might have meant nothing. To Louis Gaudin it presaged catastrophe. Yet even in the fear that seized him, he was aware that Father Baraga, still absorbed in his breviary, seemed not to have noted the change.

The south wind was no longer the steady and strong breath it had been. It was puffing. It blew and stopped, blew and stopped. In his practiced lore, Gaudin knew that this phase would be brief; it was only the warning that some much more important change impended. The single shift which might still permit of hope would be for the wind to quarter in the east. And Louis had never in all his experience known a south wind to swing directly into the east and stay there an hour. A south wind went into the east from the west and north; a west wind would blow them all over the lake, and a north wind, always a gale at this season, would swamp them surely.

But it did him no good to know with certainty what was to happen. They were now many miles from land. He had little doubt that their situation was hopeless.

Even while he considered these matters, the wind whipped out of the west. In a moment the sea was agitated. The canoe danced on the short waves and Louis had difficulty getting it unmasted. He was filled with panic and his hands, usually expert, shook and fumbled.

Now began a desperate struggle to keep the craft into the wind. Gaudin knew that they were nearer land to the west than in any other direction and their only hope was to make a westward shore before the wind veered north. If only he could manage the canoe! To turn with the wind would be to turn into the immensity of Lake Superior. The temperature would fall soon and they might have freezing weather in a few hours. Gaudin moaned and chattered. His movements were automatic now. His mind made no response when the wind again quartered, blowing from the northeast. But some instinct told him to put his back to the wind and keep it there. He had done with reasoning.

His terrorized muttering became finally articulate. In a whimper rather than a cry he said, "O mon Père, now see what we have done! Pray for us, mon Père!"

Father Baraga, sitting so that he faced forward, turned with practiced skill in the canoe to look at the voyageur. Beholding the terror on the face confronting him, he marveled at his own feeling of security. Louis suffers intense agony, he thought. I understand that. We are many miles from land and these waves are above our heads when we sink into the troughs between them. We are wet to the skin. It is becoming cold. We have no food. We have little notion where we are on this wild and frantic waste. Nevertheless —

"My Louis," he called, "I have been directed on an errand of God. Do not be afraid."

But it was impossible to allay the voyageur's terror. Again and again the priest assured him of their safety; Gaudin seemed no longer to hear him. His head sagged and he strove on with a kind of stupefied tenacity.

How long they were driven along, tossed and battered, neither knew. Each of them was past knowing, the one enervated by utter hopelessness, the other sustained by faith that lifted him above his surroundings. Yet they both recognized a change in their situation at the same moment. It pressed upon their ears — the pounding of surf upon rocks. Then they saw, when the canoe was lifted high, the white and frenzied waters boiling and seething on a jagged line of coast. No boat could survive that!

Gaudin raised his head to look at it, then slumped forward. "It is the end," he muttered.

Suddenly he roused, looked about in wild terror, seized the paddle in a last desperate grip, and cried, "Where now, mon Père? Where?"

"Straight on, my Louis, straight on!"

The surf seized the cockleshell canoe and lifted it almost upright on its stern. Its occupants clung to the sides. Spray shut out any view of their surroundings. The boom of the sea on the black rocks was deafening. Then the canoe shot forward like an arrow from a gigantic bow. Gaudin closed his eyes.

But there was no crash. The priest's voice still reached him in the calm, unbroken cadence of prayer. And now he felt the canoe in gentle, rhythmic motion. Quickly opening his eyes, he looked straight into those of Father Baraga. He knew instantly that he saw something there that he had never seen before.

"O mon Père," the voyageur cried and seized the priest's hand, pressing it to his lips. "Mon Père, we are saved!"

They were floating serenely in quiet water in the mouth of a little river. The air was warm and still. Outside their haven the sea pounded under the lash of a northeaster.

"Now, my Louis, let us erect a cross."

When two sticks crudely lashed at right angles had been set up and made secure at the base by a heap of rocks, they both knelt and prayed. Then Louis walked along the shore and looked about. When he returned he did not immediately speak to Father Baraga, but went again and stood before the cross. Removing his cap he stayed there for a long time.

At last he spoke. "I know this place, mon Père. I have been on this shore. From here we can get to Spotted Feather's village in a few hours of walking."

"That is well."

"Père Baraga, this place has no name."

"Shall we name it then?"

"I have thought of a name, mon Père — but you name it for you will have a better one."

"Oh no, Louis! It must have the name you have chosen."

"Then it is named the Cross of Baraga's Traverse!"

Father Baraga smiled.

"Let us go now to Spotted Feather's village, my Louis. We must hurry."

CHAPTER XIII

IT WAS smallpox that Father Baraga found among the members of Spotted Feather's band.

Something in the Indian's physical make-up or in his domestic habits made him peculiarly susceptible to this scourge. Among the Lake Superior natives it had been known to take off whole families, even to decimate whole bands. It did not confine itself to one locality but raged throughout an entire region, and now, the first report of it had sent Indians scattering in all directions in a mad race to leave it behind them.

Father Baraga often wished that he had schooled himself more thoroughly in the treatment of sickness. Yet his knowledg was considerable. He was not prepared to vaccinate, it is true, but he had a small stock of standard medicines which he could administer with the requisite skill. However, he could not carry a medical pack on his back during his long and dangerous journey. And there was another, more important reason why he did little doctoring. He perceived that it was futile. Unless the Indian patient was under constant observation, the administration of medicines was more likely to prove disastrous than to effect a cure. If pills were left with instructions that they be taken at spaced intervals, it was almost certain that all of them would be swallowed in one dose. Moreover, if the case took an alarming turn, the patient's relatives very often resorted privately to ancestral magic. Father Baraga had realized early that the ancient religion of these natives was still a potent influence. Troubles that they could not understand or combat led them to intensify their devotion to pagan rites. He did not waste much effort in threats or scolding at this tendency. His method was rather direct and infinitely patient teaching.

That winter, the medicine men's lodges in the villages were more active than usual. The incessant booming of drums and rattle of magic gourds, the grotesque dancing, the now-childish and now-devilish incantations over and ministrations to the desperately ill — all the heathenish practices received impetus that winter — so that Father Baraga was often depressed, and sometimes near despair.

He traveled from village to village constantly. So many times that he lost count, he knelt beside fever-wasted and pox-incrusted Indians in fetid and loathsome lodges, administered the rite of baptism and prayed. He never knew how many hundreds of miles he plodded alone over faint trails which he often lost, to come upon half-starved families marooned in the wilderness. Day after day he went on, fagged with travel, cold, hungry — days that quickly changed to nights so bitter and dreadful that he prayed almost from dusk to dawn.

Yet there were other moments, too, when he counted with gratitude the souls he had reached. When he saw the results of his teaching. A simple act of faith and good will by an Indian could lift him above the awful meanness of the life about him, and then he dwelt for a time in a place of quiet joy, where he felt the peace of God upon him as a benediction.

At midday yet two suns from La Pointe and home, he came upon a single lodge on a wide bend of the river. He had been without food for twenty-four hours and his snowshoes had become lead on legs that ached with weakness and fatigue. When he saw the lodge he thought at once of food and rest to strengthen him for the miles between this place and home.

He stumbled into the lodge and sank down upon the floor, almost wholly spent.

"Boo-zou," he whispered.

He discovered in the poor light an old man and an old woman sitting silently with their blankets close about them. Behind them in the shadows, an infant cried. Looking intently toward the sound, he made out a young woman comforting the fretting child.

"Is the child sick?" he asked.

"No, he is only hungry," the old man answered. "We have not eaten for two suns. My son is hunting. He may bring something. He has been gone a long time. We have nothing."

Father Baraga was filled with complete misery. His own needs were acute, but his thought was only, These people are starving.

[101]

"Let us baptize the child," he suggested. They readily agreed.

The people in the lodge, grown more friendly, told him over and over of their regret that they could provide no food for him. The old woman rocked back and forth and wailed faintly while her husband explained that some twenty miles farther on toward his destination, the priest might hope to find an Indian village.

Having rested, and given the little group words of encouragement, Father Baraga put on his snowshoes and resumed the weary course. In his present state he had no expectation of arriving at the village that night; he would have to sleep again in the snow without food.

He had trudged for some time at the unhurried but steady pace which the wilderness had taught him, when he thought he heard a faint call. He stopped and listened. The call was repeated, louder this time. He placed it on the trail that his own snowshoes had made. At last he saw the figure of the young mother whose child he had just baptized. She was running toward him and he turned back to meet her. The child has died, he thought. But as she approached he saw that she was smiling.

Her race after him had left her almost breathless. Her husband, the young hunter, had returned. He had killed a small deer and brought it home on his shoulders. The priest must return with her and feast.

A wave of elation swept his numb body. Here was food and lodging for the night. But more sustaining than the meat he would eat, and more comforting than companions and shelter in the long, cold night, was the act of simple charity of these people who had so little to give.

[102]

The call was repeated, louder this time.

[103]

The young hunter, a tall and handsome Indian, took great pleasure in Father Baraga's return. It was he who had sent his wife flying after the departed guest. He shook hands very solemnly but with evident satisfaction. Meat was already in the kettle over a fire, the old woman now surprisingly full of energy as she went about its preparation.

The hunter told his story while they ate. He had run the deer for two suns, sleeping on the trail and resuming the chase at daylight. For all his weariness he had maneuvered the creature into a course that would bear always toward the lodge. In the deep snow the little deer had finally become exhausted and, without expenditure of a single shot, the nearly spent hunter had dispatched it with his knife.

Arrived home after that long and arduous trip, Father Baraga found sickness at La Pointe. There had been cases of smallpox all winter but during this last absence they had increased in number. The school that Antonia was teaching for him had to be abandoned.

Seeing Antonia, he was overcome by the evidences of her sacrifice. Before she could tell him of her labors, he read them in her face. All her color was gone and her eyes burned too brightly. She was very thin and her shoulders drooped. He knew at a glance that she had overspent herself.

She had put all her energy into nursing visits from home to home. The children cried for her presence. She sat with feverish little hands in her own, soothed little bodies tossing in torment. It was her hand that had lain upon the pallid brows of many who died. Consoling the grief of mothers, anxious to get to the next place where she was so badly needed, she had forgotten to eat; while the demands upon her had made it impossible to find time to sleep. Yet the priest saw in the wan face of his sister the peace of the blessed. He could find no word to chide her.

But the spirit that had kept her going while he was absent now deserted her. The spur of duty that pushed her through the days when she must minister to Frederic's people for him, no longer pressed. She collapsed and was put to bed.

No hardship he had ever suffered compared with the feeling that overwhelmed him as he sat beside her. Was he to bury her in this cold, cheerless wilderness? To the sorrowful and exhausted man, there came one of those intervals of doubt and darkness which try the truly great of soul. The call of his mission suddenly seemed remote, almost unreal. When he looked upon his sister's face, all the details of the serene life they had known in the Suha Krajina gathered themselves into a picture of lost family happiness. He could see Amalia, the good and faithful sister who had been like a mother to him and Antonia. His desire for the comfort of her presence in this room was so intense it was almost agony. We must flee this dreadful place, he thought. Let us be restored to our birthright.

He would, he felt, have only himself to blame if Antonia died. If I had remained at home, she would not be here now. O my little sister, I hold your thin and tired hand and close my eyes to find you romping at play beside an older brother whom you adored. I have led you to this sacrifice, half around the world from the peace and happiness we knew as children. How blessed to stand again side by side in the sun and wind on the hills of a land we may never see!

The Man of Sorrows knew the utmost depths of grief, and He has ever tested and strengthened, by its searchings, the souls of His truest servants.

CHAPTER XIV

ANTONIA slowly recovered but it was evident to both of them that the strength she had paid out of her reserves would never be completely restored. Father Baraga was anxious now that she be back in the ancestral home with Amalia, for he believed her frailty indicated that she would not live long. The rigors of the Lake Superior climate were unthinkable for her.

One June night Frederic Baraga left his house at dusk and went deep into the forest. All that night he searched his soul. In the long darkness he prayed. O God, why am I here in this place where mere living is hard and dire? Might I not serve You, as Your good servant Father Zajec suggested long ago, in my ancestral land? O God, do I offend You by wanting to temper the sacrifices of my good and devout sisters? I have served You in these pastures of the wilderness for ten long years. Antonia departs tomorrow. Are we to say farewell forever? Do You ask that I remain? Have You still further work for me in this strange land?

And One told him: "As long as you did it to one of these My least brethren, you did it to Me." As the familiar words sounded in his soul, he seemed to pass from a painful dream into daylight. He knew again who he was, he felt again the full urgency of his call. His troubled will came home once more to the will of God.

The next morning he stood with Antonia on the deck of the vessel that would carry her down the lake on the start of the long journey homeward. Nothing showed on their faces except the bravery of their hearts. They understood that Antonia had given all she had to give, and that for her brother there was still work to do. Thus they bade each other farewell.

[106]

On a day late that summer of 1840, he watched a small party of travelers move up from the landing toward the fort. Surrounded by a crowd of curious natives, three white men proceeded slowly. One of them was carrying a small black and white spaniel in his arms to protect it from the half-starved native dogs that were dodging the kicks of the crowd and circling warily.

As the party neared the fort, Dr. Borup met them. Too far away to hear any of the words that were spoken, the priest saw the small man who held the spaniel pass the dog over to one of his companions and advance a step to shake hands with the factor. He heard the latter's voice raised to order the crowding natives away, and as they fell back at his command, saw his manifestations of cordial greeting to the strangers. Now he led the travelers into his office. The curious bystanders still loitered, watching the closed door.

As Father Baraga approached, Old Micho, a voyageur, discovered him. Old Micho had a love of authority that was often amusing. But he also had a reputation for mind-reading. More than once he had anticipated Father Baraga's admonitions to a crowd, sometimes even saying loudly what the priest had thought but deemed wisest not to utter. Now Old Micho sprang forward and turned to face the gaping crowd.

"It is not nice!" he cried. "Go about your business and leave decent people alone!"

Father Baraga, mingling with the crowd, smiled.

"Very well, Micho, let us all begone. Come!"

There was laughter, but the old voyageur's command and the smiling acceptance of it by the priest had their effect. The bystanders wandered away.

[107]

Old Micho walked beside the priest. He said, in a low voice, "Dose man, he axe me quick he lan' and he say, 'Micho, you fin' dat Buffalo!' "

"Now, Micho, how did he know your name?"

Micho acted a little hurt.

"I tol' heem, mon Père. I say, 'Sir, I am Old Micho!' "

Father Baraga smiled.

"You introduced yourself. That was a very kind thing for you to do, Micho."

Old Micho stopped walking.

"Dose man," he whispered, "I tink he look to fin' copper! W'at you tink, mon Père?"

"I do not know, Micho. But is not Buffalo on the Ontonagon now?"

For answer Old Micho squinted craftily, puffed his cheeks and shrugged his shoulders in the common Canadian gesture of one unwilling to commit himself.

"I guess you didn't t'ought Old Micho know somet'ing, eh, mon Père?"

"Buffalo is away and many of the young men are with him," the priest said seriously. "Micho, if you know something is going on, I want you to tell it to the factor. Is there more trouble with the Sioux?"

"Oh no, no, mon Père! But I tink dat Buffalo was go to Sault Ste. Marie." Micho made an inscrutable face and left the priest standing in the roadway.

The latter, watching him hurry off, felt a little disturbed. It was not the first time that he had heard Old Micho mention the Ontonagon copper with a mysterious, crafty light in his eyes. But now Father Baraga dismissed his misgiving, telling himself that the voyageur was merely attempting to live up to his reputation for exclusive foreknowledge.

At dusk a note was delivered to him. It announced the presence of notable guests at the factor's house and requested the pleasure of Father Baraga's company that evening, that he might supply them with information they needed about the Indians.

As he knocked at Dr. Borup's door the missionary could hear music and laughter within. When he was admitted into the brightly lighted room out of the soft, black night, he was conscious for a moment only of the animated confusion of a social gathering. As he saw more of his surroundings he felt a little uncomfortable among the lavish furnishings of the factor's parlor, and wished for a brief moment that he were back within the plain walls of his simple room. It was the first time he had been in Dr. Borup's home. He had known there was a piano, for he had sometimes heard it being played as he passed by in the street. But he had not realized that La Pointe could open a door upon a room where cultured society, fashionably dressed, would be at home. It was all in the tradition of the fur trade.

The factor was becoming expansive.

"Dr. Houghton, the fur trade will continue to be the life and business of the Lake Superior country. True, it is no longer the lucrative business it once was. But it is a natural commerce, in keeping with the country and the climate. It has two centuries of success behind it. It has built itself a great code — a code that was first introduced by men of great abilities. Now, of course, we have heard these tales of copper and silver many, many times and for many, many years. But we have taken them for what they are worth — that!" He snapped his fingers in a gesture of disdain.

It was late in the evening and only a small group of men sat talking. Father Baraga, watching the face of the alert, pleasant little man who had carried the spaniel from the landing, saw a smile form and spread as the factor spoke. The missionary liked this young Dr. Houghton. He found him intelligent, kindly and completely sincere. Ten years younger than himself and probably twenty years younger than the factor, Houghton appeared far more mature in experience and judgment than his years indicated.

Now the traveler turned to Father Baraga.

"I have discovered your influence on Lake Superior, Father. Have you too heard the tales of silver and copper?"

"I hear the tales and I see the copper and silver," the priest replied. "Objects made of these minerals are not at all uncommon among the Indians."

"And are you told the sources, the places where they are found?"

Father Baraga looked at the factor and then at Houghton.

"I am interested neither in the furs Dr. Borup trades for nor in the minerals you search for, sir. I am interested only in the salvation of pagan souls."

Douglass Houghton's face assumed an expression of abstraction. Without looking at the priest, his tone little more than a murmur, he asked, "And would you not extend your interest to include souls of men born in the acceptance of Christianity, yet lost in cupidity, in venality?" Then quickly, before the priest could answer, with a characteristic alertness he leaned forward and placed his hand on Father Baraga's arm, looking earnestly into his eyes. "I, too, Father, am an instrument of the Lord!"

Before the missionary could speak, the factor's voice had boomed forth again.

"How would you get these minerals out of the country, may I ask? Do you realize that we are a landlocked lake, sir? Do you realize that our climate is such that you could carry on your mining operations only a few months of each year? I am assuming, of course, that the minerals are here!"

Douglass Houghton looked at the factor quizzically for a long moment.

"As I have already told you, Dr. Borup," he said then, "I am the official geologist of the state of Michigan. I am charged with investigating and reporting the mineral resources of this new commonwealth. What I have found, or what I may hereafter find, will be the subject of my official report. But you fool yourself, sir, in the matter of the possibilities of developing the resources of Lake Superior. There is such a thing as American enterprise. There is such a thing as American ingenuity. I am not suggesting it either to praise it or condemn it. I suggest it as something very real, something that has had historical demonstration. As a people we are fast becoming rich and are piling up large reserves of capital. We are a restless and energetic people. We are inured to hardships. Dr. Borup, if conditions should warrant, I have no doubt whatever that a ship canal would quickly unlock this lake!"

Father Baraga had the feeling that the geologist was leaving much of his thought unspoken, and that all the important things he was saying by implication were lost on the tradition-bound factor.

"You know," the young man went on, "I came through here in 1831 with Mr. Schoolcraft's expedition. At that time we had available the reports of the treaty commissioners, General Lewis

Cass and General McKenney. They had made a treaty at Fond du Lac in 1823."

He searched among the papers of a file that lay on the table before him.

"Yes, I have the notes here. At Fond du Lac in 1823, the Ontonagon Indians seem to have been represented. During the negotiations General Cass said to the Indians, 'We also wish to look through your country and take such minerals as we may find. This copper does you no good here, and it would be useful to us in making kettles, buttons, bells and other things.'

"Then Plover, an Ontonagon Indian, replied as follows: 'I have no knowledge of any copper in my country. There is a rock there. I met some people in search of it. I told them if they took it, to steal it and not let me catch them.'" Dr. Houghton looked up from the paper and smiled. "Possibly Plover might have become a noted diplomat in different circumstances," he remarked.

"Then" — still consulting his notes — "another of the Ontonagon Indians, whose name is not recorded in the report, spoke as follows: 'You have heard the words of Plover about the rock. This, Fathers, is the property of no one man. It belongs to all of us. It was put there by the Great Spirit, and it is ours. In the life of my father, the British were busy working on it. It was then big like that table. They tried to raise it to the top of the hill, and they failed. They then said the copper was not in the rock, but in the bank of the river. They dug for it, working under the ground with a light. The earth fell in and killed three of their men. It was left till now. Fathers, at the time of which I speak, a great price was paid by the British for our permission. We expect no less of you. If you take the rock, Fathers, the benefit must be to our children who are now so high. For ourselves we care little. We are old and nearly worn out.'

"I want to explain to you," Dr. Houghton went on, laying aside his papers, "that I have twice seen this copper boulder. The first time was in 1831 when I was with the Schoolcraft party, and I have just come from a second inspection of it. It will interest you to know that some chisels we left there broken in 1831 are still there. Of course, the Cass treaty of 1823 permits us to carry away such minerals as we may find, but that would apply only to float pieces or specimens. Mining, in any real sense, will require the sinking of shafts and the removal of great bodies of minerals now well beneath the surface. Another treaty is in the making, I may disclose, by the terms of which the Indians will be expected to grant the land, perhaps with certain reserved areas, to the federal government.

"Now I have never before had an opportunity to learn the views of a man like you, Father Baraga, in whom the Indians have great confidence. It is not altogether clear what was in the minds of those Ontonagon Indians when they were treating with Cass and McKenney at Fond du Lac in 1823. How much were they saying and how much were they leaving unsaid?"

"I am sure that the unidentified Indian in your notes is Kon-te-ka," the missionary replied. "He has told me what he said at the treaty-making, in almost the same words. The Indians tried to explain to General Cass that this copper rock belongs to no one of them but to all of them alike. I believe it is very difficult for the civilized white man to understand completely what is in the Indian mind when such a statement is made. You will note that the British who came for the rock were not claiming it or buying it in the name of the British nation. No, they were procuring it as individuals. But the Indians

[113]

were selling it as a community — so much for each man, woman and child. It is my opinion that few white men really comprehend the Indian property-sense. That is certainly true of the men the government sends to deal with them. The government makes its payments in terms of individuals, but the Indians do not understand it that way. And by the same token, when the government lets one Indian starve, the whole tribe has been mistreated.

"Because the government ignores this communal sense, or fails to comprehend it, there is great misunderstanding. None of these treaties has been satisfactory to the Indians after it was made. The government is used to that and assumes that the Indians complain insincerely. But I know they are sincere. Dr. Houghton, I studied civil law in my university days and I was taught that no contract exists without a complete meeting of minds between those contracting. These treaties are contracts — but I fear that the white mind and the Indian mind have never met completely in making them. Perhaps it is impossible. They approach the negotiations with different philosophies, neither ever fully known to the other. That explains why you ask, 'How much were these Indians saying and how much were they leaving unsaid?'"

The talk went back and forth for another hour. The factor, it was evident, would continue to live in the Montreal tradition. But Dr. Houghton plied the priest with questions, and listened attentively to the answers.

In the morning Houghton called on Father Baraga, to pay his respects before departing. Together they walked slowly down to the landing.

"For a long time," the priest said, "I have been thinking

[114]

that I must find a place where I can gather my Indians and make a home for them — a permanent home where I can encourage them to better efforts in providing for themselves. The fur regime is passing, and I fear that they will suffer beyond description in the new order that is to come. In this old order the Indians are useful, and in the long run it is good business to deal with them. But in the order that I fear your official report will launch, the Indians will be unwanted, perhaps in the way. Those who are friendly will be debauched and those who are hostile will be put aside ruthlessly."

Douglass Houghton stopped on the trail and turned to face the missionary.

"Yes," he said simply.

They walked on in silence for a time until Houghton stopped again.

"Father Baraga, I am a scientist," he said. "I shall write an exactly truthful report. If I understand America, that report will bring to Lake Superior an entirely different kind of people. First of all, it will bring adventurers. It will bring men who seek to become rich quickly and easily, with no thought of the consequences. I wish I could so word my report as to keep them out. But I cannot control that. They will come in great numbers and life will be very rough. Your Indians will suffer by contact with these men."

They stood on an elevation looking down upon the lake. Both were silent.

"How long have I to prepare?" Father Baraga asked, his eyes fixed far across the wide expanse of water.

"Not long enough, perhaps," Houghton replied.

"Then I must go quickly about my Master's business! God be with you, my friend."

CHAPTER XV

IN THE spring of 1843 Father Baraga learned that the day had indeed come.

Jean Lassard had just returned from the Ontonagon.

"The copper rock is gone," he announced. "A man named Jim Paul has taken it."

"Tell me about it," Father Baraga requested.

"There is a voyageur named Nick Miniclear with this Jim Paul," Lassard explained. "They worked together in a lead mine far to the south of here. Miniclear had been on Lake Superior before. He had heard stories about the copper rock and he told them to Jim Paul. Then Jim Paul said, 'We will go and get the copper rock and it will make us rich.' I talked with Miniclear. He said they were going to find some more copper rocks. They loaded this one on a boat and it is being taken to Detroit. But Jim Paul and Miniclear did not go with it. They have built a house and they are going to stay and get rich."

Jean Lassard continued with many details but Father Baraga was not listening. He was adding this new fact to others. Over on the long Keweenaw peninsula another man had found copper. He had found it a short distance upstream from the mouth of a little brook that they called Eagle River. Other men were already arriving in that vicinity to search for copper. And Douglass Houghton was back again, continuing his investigations.

The time has come, the priest said to himself. White men have been visiting that copper rock on the Ontonagon for centuries — French, British and American. Now an American has taken it. Something has been done that will make this great wilderness different from anything man has known here. Where is my place in this future? I came to America as an Indian missionary. Shall I now persuade my Indians to move west ahead of the gathering storm, go with them beyond the last frontier and there attempt to develop and perpetuate this good beginning? The government would doubtless approve and assist. But where is this westward place beyond the frontier where my Indians might settle in peace and security? Even if such a place could be found, it would be brief sanctuary at best. I have seen the rising tide of America pushing down the Ohio, scrambling ashore on the wharves at Detroit with goods and cattle. Ever westering! Am I then looking for a place beyond the last frontier when there is no last frontier? I have been simple to suppose so. Here, in this very place where I live and work — somewhere on the shores of this lake — is the space I am seeking. For it will now become a frontier of another sort — a place where the wilderness to be conquered is not, for me, the wilderness of physical things but the wilderness of the spirit — greed, cupidity, ignorance, venality. Other men will cut down trees, dig mines, lay out roads and build cities. I also must cut away, survey and build. Here I remain!

"Ignorant!" Dr. Borup snorted. "Ignorant to the point of illiteracy! I understand this Paul has set up in business at Ontonagon. He is so crude that he thinks it amusing to refer to his place as 'Jim Paul's Deadfall.' Sir, this Paul is nothing more nor less than a roistering adventurer in cowhide boots, hickory shirt and slouch hat. He told me that he came out of the Mississippi country where men are half horse and half alligator! Those were his words, sir. He has a little cabin with a door but no window and he has set up in business! Do not ask me for an

[117]

inventory of his stock for I shall be compelled to tell you I believe it is limited to whiskey and tobacco. Yes, and vermin! The man has no reading whatever, and no manners. He spit tobacco juice all around my feet!"

"Well, he is our neighbor now, I suppose," Mr. Oakes observed.

"Neighbor!" The factor's voice showed what he thought of the idea.

"How do the Indians on the Ontonagon feel about his coming?" Father Baraga asked.

The factor sighed and rolled his eyes upward.

"He hates 'Injuns.' Those were his very words, Father. He said, 'I hate Injuns, they are all liars and thieves. But I'll have no tomfoolery from them. I claim all the land on both sides of the river here at the mouth, and these sneaking devils will take my orders or get out.' That's what this Paul told me. I said, 'Mr. Paul, these Indians have been here a long time; generations of this band have made it their home.' The fellow squinted at me and said, 'Well, I've already proved a little ownership to one of 'em with a club.' "

"What is his claim worth in law?" the priest inquired.

"That remains to be seen," Dr. Borup replied. "The government is preparing to set up a mineral agency at Ontonagon. It seems that mineral claims are to be granted to individual citizens. Several square miles to a claim, I understand. Prospectors are coming in and running all through the country. They won't find anything. If the Lord will give us the patience to stand it for a year or two, this whole mineral business will end as suddenly as it began."

Father Baraga disagreed, but he did not argue. Instead he said, "Dr. Borup, I understand that here at La Pointe we are not a part of the new state of Michigan. That state is apparently two large separated peninsulas. But the great peninsula that forms much of the south shore of Lake Superior would seem to belong geographically to the mainland that is now called Wisconsin. It seems strange to form two areas completely separated by water into one political unit."

"Yes!" Dr. Borup exploded. "And this northern peninsula is just the garret, the attic to the main building. The real Michigan is down below. Those people down there didn't want this northern peninsula but they had to take it to get into the Union of States. Look here!" The factor placed his left hand, palm down, flat on the counter before him. "That is Michigan," he declared, looking at his hand. "Detroit is down here at the base of the thumb, and in here between the hand and the extended thumb is Saginaw Bay. Up here at the tip of the longest finger is Mackinac." He looked up at Father Baraga.

The priest smiled and pointed.

"Yes, and here by your little finger is the Grand Traverse country and about here is my Arbre Croche of blessed memory. I had almost forgotten. I have traveled all those waters surrounding your hand. And I was overland to the Grand River down here on the western side. Yet I have never really known the people settled in the interior across here, the wide part of your hand. I suppose *they* are 'the state of Michigan.' "

"Well, they would have to be," the factor declared. "There are not enough people out here to make even one county."

He now turned his hand crosswise, this time keeping the thumb close but spreading the little finger wide from the others.

"See now, Father, this is the northern peninsula. It lies across the lower one, in a manner of speaking. Over here at the tip of my long finger is the Sault Ste. Marie. This wide

[119]

space here between my little finger and the others is Keweenaw Bay. Now, my little finger extending out here is the Keweenaw peninsula."

He paused a moment, looking meditatively at his hand. "Well, I suppose from accounts I hear, that about as many new settlers come into Detroit daily as there are now in this whole northern peninsula. When they adopted a state motto, what did they write, Father? 'Si quaeris peninsulam amoenam, circumspice.' They invited the world to look about — upon what? Two peninsulas? Oh no! If you seek a beautiful peninsula, look about you. What peninsula? Why, their own, of course! But don't think that I complain. I hope for the sake of my business that the settlements remain below the Straits of Mackinac. Cities and cultivated farms would soon put an end to our commercial existence. The fur trade is quite satisfied with that state motto. May it always so read!" The factor struck his fist upon the counter and glowered.

"God has His plans," Father Baraga said, "and it might profit both of us to try to anticipate this one. We have been discussing geography. A moment ago you showed me with your hand the large expanse of water called Keweenaw Bay. Will you please tell me something about that area, Dr. Borup?"

"But you have been there yourself, Father! You have seen it yourself."

"That is true," Father Baraga admitted. "But I am asking now for your knowledge and opinion of it."

"Well, sir," the factor began, "it's a place I do not personally like. It has never amounted to much. The Indians have always lived there but the place never seemed to appeal to white men. The lower bay, L'Anse, is well off the established line of travel, of course."

"Ah," the priest exclaimed and nodded.

"Pierre Crebassa has had a trading post there for quite a number of years. The Indians are extremely poor, poorer than average, I think. They get over here occasionally, as you know. I understand that they are attached to L'Anse — there's no accounting for an Indian's taste. I think it's a poor, isolated country that will never amount to anything. Besides, there's a kind of stigma upon it. I don't pretend to know the story, but it's something about Père Ménard disappearing from there a couple of centuries ago; never was heard of again. People seem to remember it all this time and to hold it against the place. Well, it's off the beaten track, so to speak. It lies along about midway between one end of Lake Superior and the other, and the bay is probably the largest on the lake. Travel both ways by-passes the lower bay, as I said. Instead of following the shoreline, people prefer to make the longer water traverse and take the portages, which are not bad, across the Keweenaw peninsula. I doubt that there's any mineral interest there. It's an out-of-the-way place, it has no future and it's got something of a bad name. Why do you ask about it?"

"Because it is to be my new home," Father Baraga replied.

"Oh, God forbid!" cried Dr. Borup impetuously.

"Yes," the priest insisted. "I am persuaded that it has all the advantages I've been seeking."

"Advantages!" the factor exclaimed. "It has nothing but disadvantages! I have told you. You asked about it and I gave you an adverse report."

"Adversity has its uses." Father Baraga smiled as he spoke the words.

The factor glared at him across the counter for a moment, then turned abruptly, went into his office and slammed the door.

CHAPTER XVI

MR. OAKES stood looking at the priest after the factor's door closed. Father Baraga had not moved from his position at the counter, and his expression had not changed.

"I am still the only priest on Lake Superior," he said. "The extent of my parish frightens me a little."

"Yes, I know," Mr. Oakes told him kindly. "Father, Dr. Borup has a great regard for you. You must remember also that Ramsey Crooks charged him with your safety when you first came to La Pointe. Your long trips away from here alone have often caused us anxiety. Now that you may leave us, Dr. Borup is upset. By the way, Father, here are some Eastern newspapers with accounts of the copper excitement. Would you like to read them?"

Acknowledging the other's kindness, Father Baraga tucked the bundle under his arm and went home. That evening, his duties performed, he spread the journals out on his table.

In a copy of the Buffalo *Morning Express* he read a letter dated from Copper Harbor on Lake Superior:*

Dear Friend: Considering how nervous I am after prospecting over the hills of conglomerate, trap and sandstone in this wild Siberian end of the world, I hope you will appreciate the amazing triumph of will over the animal propensities when I undertake, on a gun case on my knee, to fulfill my promise to write to you.

---

*This letter, which has appeared as a quotation in Upper Michigan newspapers, was purportedly published in the Buffalo *Morning Express* in 1846, month and date unknown.

[122]

This is a queer country and a stumbling-block to world-makers. Its features and construction would almost warrant the belief that it was made by another hand from the rest of the common footstool, and that the Evil One had a hand in the matter. Anyway, it is a cold, sterile region with a great, bullying, boisterous sea, subject to sudden tempests and northwest winds.

The country is bleak, barren and savage, without any signs of civilization or cultivation except bedbugs and whiskey. It is a land of dirty shirts and long beards. Everyone looks as wild and boorish as possible, and far more so than is in any way agreeable. One, a professor, too, bragged that he had not changed his shirt in four weeks. Among such dealers as there are, arithmetic is not considered a necessary accomplishment or a Christian virtue.

But this country is undoubtedly immensely rich in mineral treasure. All the statements you have seen in the newspapers are true, and yet nineteen twentieths of the whole speculation will be a total failure. Further, there is no doubt but that a small part of the valuable deposits is all that has been seen by mortal eyes, covered as it is with drift, and the most impenetrable growth of cedar, spruce and tamarac. Nothing short of clairvoyance will ever discover it.

Those working veins situate in the interior, are using oxen (after cutting roads at great cost) which are fed on hay at $55 a ton, and all else is in proportion. There is not a spear of grass on a whole eternity of this country, and an ox turned out would be certain to starve unless he could feed on shadows and moss.

On the subject of the services of such men as know a hack from a handsaw, in geology and in mineralogy, I have only to say that such, at least in pretensions, are as plentiful as blackberries. You can scarce turn a stone without finding them and, like the squaw's puppies, they are all captains.

In a Philadelphia paper he found this account:

The federal government is very willing to abet the mad scramble to begin a vast exploitation of copper and other minerals on Lake Superior. The treaty by which the Indians relinquished title to the land itself has been hurriedly brought to a successful conclusion. The Indians have reserved only very limited areas, one of which is said to be on Keweenaw Bay. Government mineral agents are established at Ontonagon and Copper Harbor and these authorities are issuing mining permits to all comers. These permits describe tracts of varying sizes up to nine miles square, depending on the political importance of the applicant. Since surveyed lines have not been run, nobody has more than a vague idea of the real location of the tracts. Scarcely anybody knows what the interior of the country is like. Dr. Douglass Houghton's report to the Michigan state legislature, while written in a restrained scientific text, has set off a half-mad scramble that is fast becoming a frenzied, hysterical rush. There is a common impulse to get rich quickly. It is backwoods mineralogy with a vengeance. Most of those who have gone to Lake Superior and returned to civilization say they distrust and hate the country but that it is undoubtedly rich in minerals.

A Detroit journal reported a traveler's account of Ontonagon:*

On the right bank, near the mouth of the river, two or three acres of land have been cleared. This clearing is covered with the tents of explorers, with only two buildings, Jim Paul's cabin and the government mineral agency. The river is full of explorers' boats. They come here to rest and replenish their stores. It is a motley crowd among which

*From an article by State Senator John H. Forster in the *Michigan Pioneer and Historical Collections*, VII, 181.

are old voyageurs, Frenchmen, half-breed Indians. These copper hunters are in truth, with their slouch hats, flannel shirts, moccasins, ironclad pants and unkempt hair, eager, determined fellows, indifferent to heat, wet, cold, hunger and toil, and with plenty of wild oats to sow. Bursting from the forest after a long sojourn, with a shout and a bound, their greetings are not of the gentlest. They take these occasions to indulge in drinking, carousing, gambling, fighting and in all manner of frontier excess.

Reading on through the newspapers he found many similar accounts of the copper rush. When he had read all of them, he extinguished the taper on his table and sat in the darkness of the room. Ever since his talk with Douglass Houghton he had been convinced that he must establish a mission post at some central location where he might concentrate many Indian families in a fixed community strong enough to serve as its own bulwark against the pressure of the new times. The two largest permanent Indian settlements were at Sault Ste. Marie and La Pointe. The first of these was too far eastward, the other too far westward. If he was to continue to regard all of the Lake Superior country as his parish, he must be centrally situated. Thus the great bay that bites deep into the northern peninsula about midway of the length of Lake Superior appealed to him as the inevitable place.

Now he was certain that he would move. The thought at once exhilarated and depressed him. La Pointe was a pleasant place and it was the only home he now knew. Well, he could return to it from time to time. Could he get another priest to come to Lake Superior? he wondered. He resolved to make the effort, at any rate. And for funds — the considerable

[125]

funds required to establish a new mission post on the scale he planned — he would write to the Leopoldine Society in Vienna.

I must take each step deliberately, he thought. After these letters asking for help are written, I shall consider that my first task is to build a new church here before I leave. It must be a larger and more substantial structure, and nearer to the fort. I have paid the penalty of inconvenience for the advantage of isolation. Why is it that I do not now fear the competition of outside influences as I once did? Have I become surer of myself? Perhaps, for am I not at this moment deciding to move closer to that great pushing mineral exploitation on the northern peninsula of Michigan? It is true that I am not afraid. How easy it would be to drift along in the peaceful and pleasant ways of life here! The factor is exasperated that I am not willing to do that. I must accept this challenge.

CHAPTER XVII

PIERRE CREBASSA, born of French and Indian parentage in the Red River country, had been sent to Montreal by his father for schooling. Subsequently, young Pierre came to Lake Superior and entered the service of the American Fur Company. In this employment he moved about in the region for several years until he was made the Company's agent at the trading post at L'Anse. Eventually he purchased the post from the Company and thereafter operated it in his own right.

[126]

One day in June, 1843, Father Baraga appeared unannounced at Pierre's store. When the priest explained his intention, Pierre immediately rearranged his own house, giving Father Baraga the best room for his priestly offices and a place of public worship.

The Crebassa trading post was on the eastern shore of the bay. Father Baraga had decided to look over the entire coast before he settled on a permanent site for his mission. So for two weeks that June he worked among the Indians near at hand, and each day Pierre took him in his canoe up and down the shore, suggesting and counseling with regard to the selection of a site.

Father Baraga finally chose a place on the west shore of the bay. Many factors determined the choice. At La Pointe his church membership had embraced many Canadians, but here on L'Anse his work was to be almost wholly with the Indians. For this new venture he desired a place well removed from the influences of any white settlement. Thus he put the width of the great bay between the mission and the trading post of Pierre Crebassa, friend though the latter was. In addition, he needed cheap land, but land that was fertile enough for the cultivation of gardens and small farms. The tract he chose was finally acquired from the federal government without cost. Again, he felt that the mission should be established at a place agreeable to the Indians themselves, so his selection was a site they often used for camping. Assinins he called it, in honor of the local Indian chief whom he had baptized and trained in religious duty, and who was to remain his devoted friend as long as he lived. And Assinins it is today, still remote from any settlement and still devoted to the charitable Christian purposes for

[127]

which it was established in a physical and spiritual wilderness a century ago.

No one knew better than Father Baraga, that summer of 1843, that the establishment of a mission station is more than the choosing of a site. Title to the land had to be acquired, and buildings erected. Indians must be persuaded to come there to live. Tillage ground must be cleared and cultivated and planted. And Father Baraga had no money.

These were his thoughts as he sat alone in the room of Pierre Crebassa's house on that first sojourn. Suddenly the door was thrown open and Pierre himself stood there.

"Come quickly, mon Père, there is a little one to baptize. It is the boy, Louis Osagi. I fear he may die."

Louis Osagi was six years old. With the family kneeling about the child on the ground, Father Baraga baptized him.

Two days later he performed another office. The little body of Louis Osagi was committed to its native soil. Standing at the head of the grave, Father Baraga had a strange experience. It was as if he was back in his own room on another continent. He was sitting at his table. Before him lay a letter that he was composing to his Bishop, and one sentence stood out clearly: "Now at length I hear from afar a voice which invites me to come to the holy mission." He looked up in astonishment. Beyond the group of silent Indians, through the trees he saw the shimmering waters of the bay. And he knew he was where he belonged.

There was no Joseph Dufault to supervise building operations here. There were none of those lovable Canadians to ply willing and expert axes. Father Baraga sighed, remembering La Pointe and his first days there when they had built him a better church in one week than he would have at Assinins after a whole year.

Money was lacking; labor was lacking. He wrote a letter to the Leopoldine Society, saying, "L'Anse is an unpleasant, sad and sterile place bearing no comparison to La Pointe. I have here no comforts, oftentimes barely the necessities of life."* He missed the friendly, garrulous Canadians who had always tried to please him. Often, indeed, he feared he was attempting to cultivate sterile spiritual soil. He remembered Dr. Borup's opinion of the place. He realized that he was discouraged — more than he had ever been in his life.

Then he told himself that true success lay only in motive and effort. The results were not really his concern. Daily, with his own hands, he worked on his church, often alone, sometimes assisted by a few Indians. These of course were unskilled workmen; they were not builders and such craftsmanship as they possessed was not with the tools of white men. There were hours each day when Father Baraga taught in the school he had started; there were hours of prayer and of ministrations. But in the long summer twilight, and sometimes by the light of the moon, he slowly erected his church.

Yet the Indians were beginning to respond. In the summer of 1844 he managed with their help to erect fifteen small log houses, each on its own measured tract of land. As the beginning of his larger plan, he selected fifteen Indian families to occupy these houses.

He was well aware that he must not attempt to impose on the Indians at Assinins the white man's definition of civilization. Indeed, he would not have done so even though it were possible. He had long recognized in these Indians certain natu-

---

*The letter was dated October 4, 1844, and written at L'Anse.

ral traits that were admirable, but he was impressed by their helplessness in the face of the white man's advance. He was appalled by their poverty. He believed that he must first teach them to be less improvident, to lay up food against the long, devastating winters. In the open months large catches of fish could be taken and salted or smoked for future use; in the fertile earth, vegetables could be grown abundantly and the surplus stored. The simple log houses would keep his Indians warmer, cleaner, and they might generally make themselves less suscepti-ble to disease. As a first step in proper development, he hoped to teach them that the summer must not be idled slothfully away. They must be helped to stand on their own feet in their simple economy and thus win an independence that would go far toward protecting them against white corruption and exploitation.

He became now something more than their priest. He saw to it that the ground was cleared and broken and planted. He provided the seeds and supervised the sowing. Much of the actual labor he himself performed.

At the end of September his church was ready to be blessed. It was a small log building lacking every gracious appointment. Even so, before it was completely finished he was in debt to the American Fur Company. But the Leopoldine Society sent him a goodly sum of money and furnished besides altar linens, a chalice, a monstrance, a ciborium, a censer. Also included in the shipment were rosaries and crucifixes.

The church was dedicated to the Most Holy Name of Jesus.

L'Anse, like La Pointe, was a place where many Indians came and went in addition to those who made a permanent home there. In the summer months great numbers journeyed to

He provided the seeds and supervised the sowing.

[131]

Sault Ste. Marie and Mackinac Island. That annual trip had been fixed in the fur trade tradition, for all of the colonial regimes had distributed presents at Mackinac. The habit of making the journey each summer persisted long after there was any important reason for it. Many of these passing Indians made short sojourns at L'Anse. Among them Father Baraga searched for any who might be persuaded to settle at Assinins.

There was also, at Lac Vieux Désert to the southward, a numerous band of Indians whose access to Lake Superior was over an ancient trail to L'Anse. These might be regarded as a detachment of the band at L'Anse, for there was a good deal of family relationship between the two groups. Father Baraga hoped to persuade some of these interior Indians to move to L'Anse.

Aloof as he was from the main current of the mineral development, he began to notice the pressure of it even on his own Indians. In all his personal experience with the fur trade, he had never seen whiskey carried to the Indians so openly, or for such despicable purposes. On one occasion the effrontery was so gross as almost to invade the very precincts of the mission station.

CHAPTER XVIII

THE success of Father Baraga's venture was not yet assured. He feared to leave Assinins even for a few days. His temporal responsibilities pressed upon him constantly during the months when land-clearing, gardening and building were possible. He was determined that winter, however severe and prolonged, should not find these Indians with too little food. While the fur catch was not likely to be great in any future season now, the hunting could still be depended upon for some certain returns, and any Indian family might reasonably expect to have a pack of furs each spring. The bay was full of fish both summer and winter, though fishing in the latter season was not always possible. Even when the shallower waters of the bay had frozen evenly so that fishing through the ice would have been pleasant and profitable, fierce storms might whip in off the wide expanse of the lake, breaking up the new ice and piling it into great windrows. Hence Father Baraga encouraged the catching of surplus fish before winter set in, and took care that the excess over immediate needs was put away. How gratified he had been, too, to see the first crops of potatoes and other vegetables stored in pits for winter use!

Actually, under his careful planning, the annual routine of Indian life was not much disturbed. The men might still go to their winter hunting grounds, leaving their families comfortably in the settlement, where the schooling of the children would continue. In the spring the reunited family would go to the sugar-making, always a gay and exciting adventure to the children. After that there was a little time for land-clearing, pending the warm days when seeds would be planted. During the summer months the cultivation of the crops and the fishing still permitted much of the leisurely life so loved by the Indians. In the autumn, the harvesting of the large gardens and the woodcutting for winter fuel took up the time until the men would depart again for the winter hunting.

Gradually the market for articles of native handicraft was increasing. The traders were beginning to buy Indian-made moccasins for sale to the prospectors and miners who found it necessary to travel in winter, moccasins being ideal footgear with snowshoes. Moreover travelers in the summer months were more numerous each year and they often bought articles as souvenirs of the country — beaded moccasins, carved and decorated pipes, gaily feathered bows and arrows.

In October of 1845 Lake Superior was swept by one storm after another. The waters of the bay lashed and pitched under the punishment of the winds. At such times Father Baraga kept indoors where he worked long hours at his writing. He had now undertaken to prepare a dictionary and grammar of the Chippewa language. A prayerbook containing some psalms had been compiled earlier.

On a day when one of these autumn storms was raging, he was in his room in the rear of the church engaged upon this work. The wind blew steadily and he could hear the sound of the surf as it rolled and broke on the wide, low beach at the foot of the higher ground on which the church stood. Under the force of the wind, rain dashed unceasingly against his little window. There was a fire in the stove and the room was not uncomfortable; the log walls had been well chinked with moss and plastered with clay. He was absorbed in his work when a blast of wind from the opened door strewed his loose papers about the floor.

Little Raven, an ancient Indian, closed the door behind him and moved over to a place near the stove. His blanket dripped water from the lower edges. While Father Baraga gathered up his papers, the old man seated himself on the floor in the warmth of the fire and brought forth pipe and tobacco. The priest was none too willing to put up with the interruption, and was not at all pleased with the smell of the rank smoke and the wet, dirty blanket in the close atmosphere of the little room. But he sensed that Little Raven had something to say to him, some message to give him when he should be ready to do so. Father Baraga did not press his guest but returned to his table and resumed writing.

After a long silence Little Raven began. "It is very bad weather."

The priest agreed and continued to write. There was another long pause.

"It is very bad weather on the lake."

Again the priest assented, writing steadily. He had almost forgotten his visitor before Little Raven spoke again:

"A man was lost."

Father Baraga was instantly attentive. He assumed that the old man referred to one of his own people. His questions were rapid.

"No," the Indian told him, "it was not on the bay. It happened two suns ago."

This was irritating, but the missionary was so familiar with the Indian character that he waited, knowing the old man would explain only in his own good time. Little Raven was indulging in a fumerie — the inevitable pipe — and in the ceremonial slowness beloved of his race. Since the tragedy was of two days' standing, and there was no immediate urgency, Father Baraga turned again to his work.

"It happened on the lake off the mouth of Eagle River," his informant offered at last. "It was that man who broke the rocks with the little hammer."

[135]

This was no identification at all. The priest had seen many geologists with that tool of their profession. He went on writing.

"It was that man with the little dog."

Instantly a picture of the scene at La Pointe years before appeared to the priest. Could it be Douglass Houghton who was lost?

"That man was a chief," Little Raven was saying. "He was the chief of all those men who made straight lines in the forest with an iron chain."

"Tell me at once, Little Raven, was that man's name Douglass Houghton?"

"That was his name," answered Little Raven.

Father Baraga took up his pen but he did not write. His sense of personal loss when he remembered the fine young scientist, blended in his mind with another experience, a deepening awareness of the issues in his own life.

Where and when God chose to end Douglass Houghton's mission is not important, as it will not be important where and when He chooses to end mine, Father Baraga thought. That he had a mission Houghton well understood; I saw the inward knowledge in his eyes. He was an unusual man because he saw all of his mission, not, as many men do, merely a small part of it. He understood that, as his mission succeeded, mine would be made more difficult. For this great wilderness will disappear and all the outward signs of man's civilization will spring up everywhere. It was given to Douglass Houghton to point to this remote, almost forgotten country and say, "Here is opportunity." When he had done that his work was finished. God brought me half around the world, forewarned me through Douglass Houghton himself as to what was about to happen.

Plainly, my mission is not finished. What was it that Douglass Houghton asked me? He asked me if I would not extend my interest to include men born in the acceptance of Christianity but who had lost all practice of it. Yes, I see more clearly now that that is part of my mission. Little Raven has brought me a message he is not aware of. There is a duty now that I must acknowledge and perform. I shall go to the mining settlements, one after the other. There are souls there who need me. God give me strength!

He decided to go to Lac Vieux Désert before he attempted the trip to the Keweenaw peninsula. The scattered and vulnerable situation of the Indians prompted him to seek out the band there with the immediate hope that they could be persuaded to join his colony at Assinins. Lac Vieux Désert is a small inland lake about fifty miles as the crow flies from the head of Keweenaw Bay. The Indians there were, even by Indian standards, miserably poor.

Father Baraga's problem was to keep his L'Anse Indians as closely at home as possible. While their blood relatives lived at Lac Vieux Désert, they had an excuse for wandering away, and he had long since noted that after they returned from these visits they were much less ardent in their religious duties. The fact was that the isolation of these inland natives allowed them to continue many heathenish practices now almost forgotten by their L'Anse cousins. The missionary had been told of rites at Lac Vieux Désert that shocked him. He wanted to bring those pagans to Assinins within hearing of his church bell, where he was certain he could win them to Christian belief and Christian living.

[137]

There was a well-defined trail from the bay to the inland lake, but because it took the easier way, avoiding hills and swamps, it made the distance to be traveled a good seventy-five miles. That trail Father Baraga took alone soon after Christmas. It was not an unpleasant journey except that his desire to arrive at Lac Vieux Désert on the second day made it necessary for him to push along unflaggingly through the daylight hours. The intervening night he spent in the open, wrapped in his blanket behind the shelter of a windbreak.

Lac Vieux Désert was a lovely expanse in the winter landscape, its shores heavily wooded down to the very edge of the water.

But if he was delighted by the scene, he was appalled by the desperate poverty and indescribable filth of the Indians living there. Some of the members of the band knew him, had seen him at L'Anse. His first business was to attend the sick, of whom there were several. While doing this, he let it be known that he desired to meet all of the people in a central lodge where he might confer with them.

He addressed them simply and directly: "My children, you are very poor at Lac Vieux Désert. You have lived here long and you do not find much game when you hunt. You often have nothing to eat unless you can take a few small fish from the lake. I want you to come to L'Anse where each of you may have a house to live in and a garden to cultivate. At L'Anse your children will be taught in the school, and you yourselves may come to church to be instructed in the word of God. If you live at L'Anse you will not be hungry, as you are here. You and your children will be happier there."

He elaborated the theme, though he had sensed a hostile reaction from the very beginning of the meeting. He suspected that two old medicine men were covertly passing word among the band to refuse the invitation. When he was certain that he had identified his opponents he addressed himself directly to them.

"We do not like to live in houses," one of them responded.

"Very well, you need not," said the priest. "No one need live in a house if he does not wish to do so. You may erect your own lodges. Many of your L'Anse brothers live in lodges."

"Indian men do not plant gardens," the other old man said.

"Very well, let your women plant the gardens while the men hunt and fish. But it is very bad to be hungry. It is not right for you as fathers to let little children cry for want of food. The children themselves, if you are at L'Anse, can help with the gardens."

He did not lose patience, though time and again during the talk he was greatly provoked. He realized that he could not immediately persuade adults to give up age-old habits. But he was certain that the objections over which they argued hour after hour were not the determining reasons why his offer was being refused. Very well, he would welcome the few who indicated they would like to come, and he would continue to hope that other recruits could be gained at a later time.

He extended his journey beyond his original plan. He had not intended to go farther than Lac Vieux Désert, but suddenly he made up his mind to push on to Lac du Flambeau. That trip was equally discouraging.

When he finally returned to Assinins, he had traveled more than three hundred miles. Nevertheless he set out within a few days for La Pointe and Fond du Lac. That journey took him seven hundred miles, and it was late in March before he again saw the wide expanse of the bay.

[139]

Not yet had he found time to make the trip to the Keweenaw peninsula which he had contemplated for so long. Always it was the Indians who claimed — and received — his first attention.

CHAPTER XIX

IT WAS just three years since Father Baraga had started the L'Anse venture. The little church fitted the frontier on which it stood — a crude edifice without embellishment. Clustered about it were some thirty small log houses with gardens. The many Indian lodges along the shore were likewise part and parcel of the community. Altogether, just less than one thousand souls were attached by varying degrees of loyalty to Assinins. Of these not more than a score were Canadians.

He often wished that he could spend all of his time with the children in the school. He had secured the services of a literate Canadian, and his multifarious duties forced him to leave most of the instruction in secular subjects to this bright young man. But when Father Baraga could put in a day at the school, it became something more than a school. He had taught the children to sing and this was one of their most enjoyable pursuits.

One day in July, 1846, the propeller "Independence" stood out in the bay before the mission station and a small boat was lowered. Bishop Lefevre of Detroit was paying his first visit

[140]

to Assinins. Ashore, the excitement was great. All the people ran down to watch, and guns were brought out and fired. It was a holiday, with the dedication of the church and the administration of Confirmation in prospect.

But there was something else, too. That tour of the Bishop's was especially devoted to the cause of temperance, and he carried the cause into Father Baraga's little community. This was no new crusade. Indeed, the fight against liquor traffic with the Indians went back to the Jesuits and Cadillac. The problem had been discussed in Montreal and in Paris. It was a long and often bitter struggle between the Church and the governors and traders.

Father Baraga recalled a long talk he had had in Detroit with Father Gabriel Richard soon after he had come to America. He learned then the whole long history of the struggle, for Father Richard knew it well. The Detroit priest had been so impressed by the extent of the liquor traffic and its dire results, that he had made a thorough study of it in all its ramifications. He related that at one time he had seen two hundred barrels of whiskey, the cargo of one vessel, unloaded at Mackinac. He had watched while the shipment was converted into "fur trade whiskey." Into an empty barrel were poured several gallons of water and then enough whiskey almost to fill the barrel. To this were added large quantities of red pepper and cheap tobacco. It was now "Indian whiskey." It cost, Father Richard said, about five cents a gallon and it was exchanged in trade at a value of two dollars a gallon. He said he knew few Indians, aside from those who had become Christians, who would not have traded for it at any price. The Indian desire for intoxicants was peculiar and inordinate, the women sharing it equally with the men.

[141]

"God alone knows how many evils flow from this traffic," Father Richard had told him. "There is something about the combination of an Indian and whiskey that is particularly vicious." And the traffic had never abated, notwithstanding the laws of France, England and the United States.

The Bishop presented to the L'Anse Indians, as he had done at all the mission stations on the lower lakes, a printed pledge in their own language: "I renounce entirely and forever the use of intoxicating liquors, and I pray God that He may give me His grace to keep this promise." These pledges were duly signed with the marks that were the Indians' signatures.

Father Baraga did not deceive himself. He knew that many of the pledges would be broken. But as he filed them away he realized that a situation was now created in which each Indian's case became separate and individual. It gave the missionary, for each of his charges, a starting place from which he could discuss personal moral responsibility. He hoped, by the grace of God, to make a little progress.

On a Sunday that summer, shortly after the Bishop had departed, a traveler attended Mass. Father Baraga noticed him, observing that he was a man of evident character. The stranger, he was soon to learn, was Philo Everett.

The number of people traveling on the lake and the important trails was increasing. Many of them stopped at the mission station for information or rest. Father Baraga enjoyed talking with these men. In some he thought he recognized the future leaders of the new country they were building, and among them men like Everett and Peter White, though not of his Faith, became his firm friends for life. Talking with such travelers raised the missionary's spirits, for he discovered in

[142]

them clean, straight concepts of life and true nobility of character. He became persuaded that when the shouting and the tumult of the mineral rush was over, spiritual fineness such as these men showed would come to the fore and a community would finally be built in this great peninsula upon the foundations of true virtue.

Great honors were to come to Peter White as a reward for his civic endeavors in industry, in government and in philanthropy; and Philo Everett was to be credited with the discovery and opening up of the Marquette iron range. They were to stand close beside their friend, the missionary Bishop, to see him lay the cornerstone of a cathedral in a city which was nothing more than a vision in the minds of all of them. Peter White was to say one day, as he stood beside a ship canal that had opened an industrial empire, "We may pause in wonder that so few and so feeble a people, living under so cold a sky, should have been permitted to share so largely in changing the seat of empire and enlarging the happiness of mankind."* And these men, on a bitterly cold January night in 1868, in a city that did not exist that summer when Philo Everett first met the missionary, were to have revealed to them another and a different empire by the Bishop who was their friend.

After Mass that Sunday, the stranger approached the priest and introduced himself. He said that he had enjoyed the singing and was agreeably surprised that Indians could sing so well. He commended Father Baraga for his achievement, and thanked him for the opportunity of attending a religious service in the wilderness. Everett himself was on a business errand to the gov-

---

*In a speech at the celebration commemorating the fiftieth anniversary of the opening of the Soo Canal at Sault Ste. Marie in 1905. The tonnage passing through the Soo Canal, open only about seven and a half months a year, is greater annually than that of the Panama and the Suez Canals combined.

[143]

ernment mineral agency at Copper Harbor. The iron deposits east of L'Anse in the vicinity of Carp River were his particular interest. His party, much in need of rest, had camped on the beach and he had decided to walk to the mission station and attend the service at the church.

The traveler spoke of the Indians in a friendly way and told how an Indian had taken him to a large deposit of iron for which he had been searching many weeks in vain.

"Then you are convinced, Mr. Everett, that the mineral is abundant and that it will bring people into those parts?"

"Oh yes, unquestionably!"

"So that we shall have the copper rush on one side of us here at L'Anse and an iron rush on the other?"

"That appears to be the situation," Everett told him, and launched into a glowing prediction of the future. It would be necessary to build a canal around the falls at Sault Ste. Marie. Larger vessels than any now on Lake Superior must be enabled to pass directly between it and the lower lakes. Many thousands of men would be required to perform the labor in connection with the copper and the iron mines. These men with their families would require schools and churches. Entire cities would have to be built. Steam railroads would have to be constructed.

"But I have been talking for an hour, Father! I must return to my camp at once. Thank you again for your kindness. This country needs you. You must continue your efforts for these poor Indians. I am afraid if you don't, no one else will."

All that day Father Baraga went about his duties with the feeling that Mr. Everett's visit would have an important bearing on his future work. He began to understand that, while he had been absorbed in his L'Anse mission, he had missed much of what was happening all about him — that the great historical current which was a young nation marching across a continent had at last caught this Lake Superior country in its sweep. He himself had come upon the lake and beheld its mode of life in the last halcyon days of a fading tradition. He thought of the many idyllic days at La Pointe when he had been testing himself, turning over and over in his mind a problem that seemed very simple to him now. But he feared he had not the requisite drive, and he knew he had little heart, to become part of the rushing, pushing tumult that was crowding in upon him. What he had to do he desired to do humbly, inconspicuously.

There were others on Lake Superior now who sought in their own way to help the Indians — men of other Faiths. He did not doubt their sincerity. Across the bay from Assinins lived the Reverend John Pitizel in a Methodist mission station. During the Bishop's visit Mr. Pitizel had sent an invitation to Assinins for Bishop Lefevre and Father Baraga to dine with him. They had accepted the invitation and had had a pleasant visit at the Protestant mission.

Now Father Baraga sat down at his table and wrote a letter:

Reverend John Pitizel, and the whole community of the Methodist Mission, L'Anse —

Dear Friends:

I have been requested to let you have the bell which is hanging in my steeple here, as soon as another one, which is now at the Sault, shall be brought to this place. But this bell does not belong to me; it was lent to my chapel by the deceased Mrs. Cotte, to whom it belonged.

As Mrs. Cotte is now no more, I have requested her afflicted husband to let you have the bell in regard of the kind services which some of you bestowed upon his lamented wife in her last days; and he cheerfully consented to give you the bell for the use of your chapel as soon as mine shall be brought from the Sault.

Your sincere friend,

FREDERIC BARAGA

L'Anse, April 7, 1846

CHAPTER XX

IT WAS one of those October days by which the Lake Superior climate redeems itself: hazy, benignly warm, sublimely peaceful. A party of Indians from Fond du Lac, traveling homeward from a summer sojourn at Mackinac, put in at L'Anse to rest and visit. While they were paying their respects to Father Baraga, it occurred to him that their coming gave him an opportunity to revisit La Pointe and Fond du Lac. When he suggested this, his callers were delighted.

His decision was quickly made, but he could not know what was in store for him.

The party resumed the journey on the lake, with Father Baraga as an honored passenger. The kindly autumn weather continued. They put in briefly at La Pointe, where the missionary promised to spend a few days with the people on his way

home. Still the good weather held. At Fond du Lac the rejoicing over his arrival made him chide himself for delaying so
long to come back to these cordial souls.

There was much to do at Fond du Lac. Numerous short
trips to outlying places used up several days of his time. Moreover, he found among these old friends and acquaintances a response to his teachings so earnest, so sincere, that he had the
impulse to lengthen his stay, and put off the thought of the long
journey back to L'Anse. Once when he did mention it, Pierre
Cotte implored him to remain. Finally, the season having worn
on, he could not deny the pleas that he stay at Fond du Lac over
Christmas, for his friends reminded him that he had never
assisted them to celebrate this holyday.

Thus it was early January when he found himself at last on
snowshoes, facing the long trail home. With him was his old
friend, Louis Gaudin.

The two set forth on an overland route at daylight of a
fine morning under the most favorable of conditions for winter
travel. The temperature was freezing — just comfortable in
view of the steady pace on the trail. The snow was firm under-
foot. Their packs contained provisions for three days, amply
sufficient to allow them to reach La Pointe. They carried also
their blankets and Father Baraga's Mass kit. Gaudin shouldered
two-thirds of the load and would have carried all of it had the
priest permitted. They planned to camp two nights, arriving at
La Pointe the evening of the third day. This schedule required
that they push along at good speed during all of the daylight
hours.

The first night out they camped comfortably, but already
there were premonitions of bad weather. When they rose at
dawn it was snowing, with a rising wind.

It was well into the second day when Gaudin suggested that they stop and prepare a meal. The storm had been steadily increasing in velocity and the heavily falling snow was blown by the wind. There was a little delay in getting a fire started, but it was accomplished and the food was soon cooked. Father Baraga was surprised to see that Gaudin ate very little, for he himself was hungry. But the voyageur said nothing and they pushed on once more.

Less than an hour had passed when the priest noted that his companion's pace had slowed. Gaudin was breaking the trail, and Father Baraga now offered to take his turn at this more arduous task. The offer was made in good faith, but when Gaudin did not refuse it, Father Baraga realized that he had expected him to do so. This is not like Louis Gaudin, the priest told himself. Yet he remained silent. Well he knew the stiff pride of the Lake Superior Canadian in his physical prowess.

Father Baraga's efforts at breaking the trail slowed the pace even more. His snowshoes sank in the new, loose snow and he soon began to tire. Yet he observed that Gaudin lagged even at this retarded pace. Waiting for his companion to come up to him, the priest saw the sweat standing on Gaudin's face in great beads. Strong misgivings arose in Father Baraga's mind. The air was becoming much colder and even in the shelter of the timber the wind lashed their faces with snow that stung and hurt. Quick glances over his shoulder had told him that Gaudin was lagging more and more. Now the priest turned back to face him. The man was staggering, weaving in and out of the trail. Father Baraga hurried back. Just as he reached the swaying figure Gaudin fell prone, his face buried in the loose snow.

Father Baraga had to use all his strength to turn the unconscious man on his back. The snowshoes caught and held as if

[148]

It took all his strength to turn Louis on his back.

[149]

anchored; the priest's fingers were numb with cold as he struggled to remove the voyageur's pack. But at last he had him over. Gaudin's face was as white as the new snow. The priest crouched beside him, and he opened his eyes.

"How is it, my Louis?"

Gaudin shook his head as though to clear his senses. At last he spoke weakly.

"It is nothing, mon Père. Let us go on." And he attempted to rise.

Father Baraga restrained him, urged him to rest, reassured him. He got out a blanket and wound it about the huge body. Slowly Gaudin seemed to grow stronger. Again he proposed that they resume the journey.

"No, let us make camp here, my Louis. I shall cook some food and the rest and nourishment will fortify us for the trail tomorrow. There is no need to hurry."

In the end that was what they did. The priest found a suitable camping site near at hand, a fire was started and Gaudin was rendered as comfortable as possible. No reference was made to his illness as the camp was prepared for the night. But in the hours that followed, fever and chills swept over him intermittently. Father Baraga had no medicines. He remained awake, dozing only at the moments when Gaudin fitfully slept.

Again and again through the night the missionary pondered their problem. He was certain that no Indians lived in the vicinity. Might he leave Gaudin here, in as sheltered a situation as he could arrange for him, and go on alone to La Pointe or back to Fond du Lac for help? He estimated that they were now about half the distance between the two settlements. But fear smote him. In the storm could he be certain of finding this place and leading men to Gaudin quickly? The trail would be obliterated. And what if Gaudin died here alone while he was gone? Yet how long could he stay here, watching over his sick companion? This, he was certain, was no quick, passing illness. And their provisions were not sufficient for long.

In his dilemma, his feelings, as he listened to the labored breathing of his companion, were tuned to a high pitch. If it were himself sick here in the wilderness, he would have no fear, no great anxiety. Of the number of the days left him for his mission he had no question to ask. But Louis! O my great-hearted child! You have loved me and served me with a devotion that has earned its own reward. You and I have faced death together, and I know your desire to live. Even now, lest my heart be made anxious, you have fallen on the trail, struggling to continue. All the sinews of this great, powerful body are racked by chill and fever, and they have borne the loads and performed the labors of your priest with simple faith and loving-kindness. Hear me, O Lord; let me bring him to safety!

At daybreak Louis insisted that he was able to go on. Father Baraga regarded him carefully. He had no better solution of their problem.

Gaudin could take no food. He staggered to his feet. Still, he insisted on shouldering the heavier pack. His teeth were set tightly together, the sweat started on his face. Fixing his gaze far ahead he stumbled forward with a silent determination that was heart-rending.

Father Baraga broke the trail with a slow, easy pace, adjusting it so that Gaudin could keep close behind. Yet they had gone but a short way when Gaudin surrendered his pack without protest. More and more frequently after that, the priest stopped and supported the reeling man to let him rest and gain strength to go on. Breaking the trail, carrying all the baggage,

[151]

supporting the heavy, helpless figure for long intervals, Father Baraga was astonished at his own endurance.

They plodded on and on. The priest's thoughts became a refrain: Keep moving, keep moving.

Now the sick man babbled in a walking delirium — unintelligible mutterings, insane raving and shouting. Sometimes he fought the frail priest who tried to keep him from falling into the deep trap of the snow.

Father Baraga staggered under the weight of the packs but he did not dare to cast them aside for in them were food and blankets. His legs were numb from fatigue. The wind whipped the snow into swirls that momentarily blinded him. He felt the pinch of frost in his feet. God, have mercy! Give us strength!

They could not travel far in one day. When Gaudin's mind was clear he would plead with Father Baraga to leave him and save himself. They rested frequently, the missionary wrapping the sick man in his blanket and waiting beside him. It required the last of Father Baraga's strength to make camp at night. Food he prepared only once a day, for himself. Louis could not eat, and was becoming weaker and weaker. Now the priest would not have dared even to consider the possibility of leaving him and making a quick dash for La Pointe. He was fearful that Gaudin would wander off in delirium and be lost.

Camp and wait. Move on. Camp and wait. There was no more food. Father Baraga calculated that on some days they made less than five miles. They had been going — how long? He tried to remember — seven, eight, nine days.

And then, in the distance, he saw men fishing through the ice. He cried out to them with all his strength. But his voice was too feeble — they were too far off. Plod on then, a little further. Perhaps the men would see before they heard.

When they came running up, Father Baraga was holding Gaudin's whole weight, trembling beneath it.

"Take him, my friends, he is very sick."

"Père Baraga, you —"

"No, no, I am able to manage for myself. I am strong. Take Louis quickly!"

He watched them lift and carry Gaudin to a sled. He watched them running across the ice toward the fort. Now they were gone. He stood swaying, waiting for sufficient strength.

O Father, Thou hast delivered Thy humble servant!

CHAPTER XXI

THREE classes of people, according to the motives that brought them, made up the growing population of the copper-mining district.

The first class, numerically small, was composed of men who were interested in the development almost solely from a money viewpoint — as a place to invest capital on the expectation of enormous profits. For the most part they were men from Eastern states with some educational attainments, at least in financial and commercial fields. Of them, Father Baraga saw little.

A second class was made up of adventurers, who were in the new mining district for excitement and to make quick, easy money. Not a few of these had found it advisable to leave their former homes between one sun and another. At first they expected to get rich directly through mining. They were soon disabused of that idea, but they continued to operate where they believed some smart, sharp practice might bring sudden wealth. These were the men Father Baraga was so anxious to keep away from his Indians.

The third class were primarily laborers, working honestly, saving their wages to establish their families in new homes here. Many had already brought their wives and children. Their economic position before the district was stabilized was not a happy one. This was the class of which Father Baraga saw a great deal.

During the rush years countless mining ventures were started and abandoned, the laborers going unpaid for months, or sometimes never paid at all. Few indeed were the early mines that could pay operating costs out of their earnings. Hundreds of attempts to develop mines failed. The money that went into these projects was Eastern capital, though not many of the shareholders of these wildly speculative mining companies were wealthy. When a wealthy man with ample capital could be induced to invest, he came in on his own terms and sooner or later owned the property completely. For the rest, it was Eastern citizens of limited means who bought a few shares of stock apiece under the optimistic persuasion of a promoter. Most of them knew nothing about their "mine" except what the promoter told them. Often one of their number would be sent to view the property and report to them when he returned. He would find a small crew of men sinking a shaft or driving an adit. It was quite inevitable, to his mind, that out of the working should come rock impregnated with copper. Mining jargon would flow and eddy about his ears; there would be talk

of "trap" and "conglomerate." Having himself shown a willingness to speculate when he purchased his own stock without
seeing the property, and being persuaded by this view of the
ground that only more capital was required to extend the scale
of the operation to the huge dividend stage, he would give a
report to his friends at home that was sure to fire their hopes
anew, and bring more money to the company.

In such a system of financing, the laborers suffered. The
pay was none too high even when they got it. The men lived
with their families in small log houses built either by themselves
or by the mining companies. Small gardens and abundant wood
fuel, free except for the labor of cutting it, made it possible to
be comfortable enough in frontier fashion. But when the employing company could neither manage credit any longer for
the workers, nor pay them their wages in cash, they were bound
to suffer.

Under these conditions no churches were built. Until a mine
could amply prove that it was capable of producing copper in
profitable quantities, everything done at that location was done
in a temporary and experimental manner. Even the laborers
were compelled to understand that their situation was transient.

It was to serve these poor people that Father Baraga went
from L'Anse, visiting many of these scattered and always isolated settlements.

Almost from the beginning, many Irish miners were attracted to the new copper country. Some came directly from
Ireland where they had been recruited by labor agents; others
were signed up as they arrived at American seaports. German
immigrants too found new homes under the same circumstances.
There came also Canadians, drifting to the new settlements
from older communities on Lake Superior. In the case of most

of these people, generations of their ancestors had lived and died in the Faith. They needed the services of a priest, and often that need was sore. The Europeans had lived mainly in small communities centered about a parish church; now they were living in small communities centered about a hole in the earth.

Father Baraga knew that he had been overly long in making the trip to the mining district. Yet he was forced to admit to himself, when he faced the situation squarely, that in his tremendous parish he was always overly long in arriving at the many places where he was needed.

The route was northerly, along the west shore of the bay to the entry to the Keweenaw waterway and thence by and across that waterway into the northernmost tip of the Keweenaw peninsula. In summer much of the distance could be traversed by canoe; in winter the whole was a snowshoe journey. After a trip or two, as his acquaintance widened, the fervent requests for his presence at more frequent intervals persuaded him to make almost impossible promises that he nevertheless forced himself to keep.

He had two friends in cabins along the route. One, called Petit Jean, lived near the entry. The other, Canadian Richard, lived at the northern end of Torch Lake, which is part of the Keweenaw waterway. If the service these two men rendered Father Baraga was crude and awkward, it was nonetheless kindly and devoted service. They had no comforts to share with him. Their cabins were mere huts and their provisions were always meager. But when he stopped to visit them, all that they had, including their lives if need be, was his.

One night in summer the missionary arrived at the cabin of Canadian Richard in a terrific thunderstorm. Declaring it the occasion for a feast, Richard used all his provisions and all his culinary skill in preparing a proper banquet for his honored guest. But he discovered as the preparations went forward that he had no "seasoning," which the priest supposed to be salt. What to do? Then he remembered that a small party had camped some distance down the waterway. Against Father Baraga's vehement protest, Richard went to his boat, moored in front of the cabin, and set off in the heavy downpour. Father Baraga could hear him singing far down the lake. In time he returned. He was excited, elated. Now he had "seasoning"! The kettle of fish soup he had cooked was waiting for it. It was maple sugar. With many proud flourishes he proceeded to shave the sugar into the soup.

Once Father Baraga stumbled into Petit Jean's cabin so exhausted that he did not know for many hours where he was. He had left a small mining location near Eagle River in the early morning. The air was still and frosty and the moon gave a soft, diffused light that made the forest seem unreal and beautiful. He was homeward bound and he thought that he had never traveled so easily and so fast as he did while the moon set and the sun rose on a still, cold world.

But before he reached Torch Lake all the portents he had come to recognize in the Lake Superior country told him that a storm was imminent. He decided against taking shelter at Canadian Richard's cabin near-by, for he was confident he could outmarch the blizzard. This proved to be an almost fatal mistake in judgment.

"Coming out of the forest, I saw myself obliged to cross the large frozen lake," he wrote afterward in a letter to a European correspondent.* "The wind was blowing straight into my face.

*The Leopoldine Society; the letter is dated, September 1, 1849.

It was a terrible blizzard. It was so violent that it almost threw me over, and so cold that it was freezing the blood in my veins. Besides, I often lost my direction as I was obliged to follow a direct line because there were no trails. I could not see ten steps ahead. Swirls of snow were wrapping me in a thick cloud and in this tumult I had to make eighteen miles with my snowshoes on."

Repeatedly he turned his back to the sharp knives of the wind while he nursed his face and rested his eyes. As he approached Keweenaw Bay the punishment seemed more than he could endure. He decided to leave the open way and seek such shelter as the timber afforded. Yet in doing this he feared he would miss the cabin of Petit Jean.

He did not know how long he withstood that terrific buffeting. He realized only that he was stumbling on blindly, relying on instinct to keep him on his course. He did not know that he had reached Petit Jean's door. He was unable to open his eyes, for his eyelids were swollen shut.

The settler, hearing something at his door, opened it to discover the priest fallen in the snow. He dragged the all but unconscious man into his cabin and put him to bed.

"The skin of my face fell off like the fabric of a vestment that is worn out," Father Baraga wrote in his letter.

He sat in his room working on his book. Dusk was falling; it was time to light a taper to finish the day's stint of writing. He looked up to discover his Canadian schoolteacher placing a note before him, which he said had just been left by a man who was even now on his way across the bay to Crebassa's. It was a cry of distress from a young mother at one of the isolated min-

The priest had fallen in the snow before Petit Jean's door.

ing settlements. Her little boy was dying, and she begged the missionary to come to him.

Within the quarter-hour, with night approaching, Father Baraga started alone on a sixty-mile journey on snowshoes through the wilderness.

What things are valuable? How shall we measure what that kind and gentle countenance meant to the young mother? How shall we weigh reward? We can only see the swift flight of a frail figure under the stars in a race through a silent wilderness to the place where a woman kneels beside the bed of her first-born. It is a poor log cabin thousands of miles from all she has ever known of comfort and serenity. She interrupts the telling of her beads to listen to the sound of feeble breathing. The hours run, the breath is faint. The anguish of the mother is unbearable. Yet ever that swift, untiring figure approaches on his errand of God.

A gentle hand rests on the kneeling woman's head. Upon the cot the flame of life flickers. A low, sure voice intones the ancient holy words.

It is a long way back to L'Anse.

CHAPTER XXII

IT WAS a decade and a half since Frederic Baraga had first come to Lake Superior. That time had been quite evenly divided between La Pointe and L'Anse. At his arrival, Lake Superior was a quiet bayou past which swept the mighty current of events that made the history of a people taking over a continent to build a nation. Then he had observed the peaceful waters made just a little restless by stray eddies from the main stream beyond. Now, at the half-century mark, he was to see the bayou inundated by the great current itself.

The forces of that current, economic, social and political, constituted a threat to the Indians on Lake Superior. In reality they were forces created by the aspirations of a multiplying people destined to demonstrate on a gigantic scale both the strength and the weakness of popular government. They were inevitable and overwhelming; they struck and passed, leaving in their wake the wreck of a dispossessed race.

As though in collusion with these human forces, a series of natural disasters came upon the Lake Superior Indians.

In the domestic life of the Indians, nature contributed directly. On Lake Superior two grains and a vegetable made a large contribution to the food supply. These were wild rice, maize and the white potato. Dependent though they were on these foods, the Indians did not put forth any very great effort to cultivate them as crops. The little that was done fell usually to the women.

Before Father Baraga took them in hand at L'Anse, the Indians had never attempted to clear land and prepare it for careful planting. Left to their ancestral practices, the Indian women dropped seeds into shallow holes in whatever loose soil they could find. Usually these casual sowings were on the banks of streams, often at the dry edges of beaver meadows. A sharp stick and a handful of seeds were the only equipment.

In the Indian economy potatoes were a perishable food. The crop was eaten as it matured, and was exhausted well before the family left for the winter hunting grounds. As for

[161]

maize, hardy though it was, it did not produce abundantly in the Lake Superior latitude. The immature ears were eaten as a sort of luxury, boiled with meat or fish.

But there was one crop that was far more important than maize or potatoes. It was the wild rice. In good seasons it gave the Indians an abundant supply of nourishing food. It was not too bulky to be carried along as the family moved from place to place, and it could be kept indefinitely. A family that took in a good harvest of wild rice was well fortified against the long, rigorous winter.

The rice grew in the marshy margins of rivers and small inland lakes in water just deep enough to float a canoe. The plants were well rooted in the oozy muck of these marshlands and grew just high enough above the surface of the water to permit quick, easy harvesting of the ripe grain. In the autumn the women gathered it. The canoe was paddled into the rice field, the heads of the plants were bent over the side and the ripe, loose grain was shaken or pounded out. Taken back to the lodge, it was thoroughly dried, poured slowly in the wind to blow away the husks, and then stored in skin sacks.

There were not many articles of food in the Indian diet. It is commonly supposed that they had an abundance of meat. As a matter of historical fact, they had little of it. The popular belief that deer were easily taken is erroneous. Deer are much more numerous in the environs of Lake Superior now than they were a century ago. The animal population rises and falls with its food supply, and in the natural conditions of the primitive forest the food supply of deer is limited. They thrive after the removal of the original forest. The Indians had venison oftener in summer than in winter, because it was easier to travel by waterways to the grazing grounds. But in summer meat does not keep. And that is one of the reasons why Indians gorged themselves, living a feast-and-famine existence.

Fish, too, were easily caught in summer but taken in winter only with great difficulty and hardship.

Father Baraga had studied these problems and his project at L'Anse was an attempt to train his people in a kind of fore-handedness that used all the natural advantages and eliminated as many of the disadvantages as possible. But his field of influence was limited to the Indians immediately settled about his mission station. And even with them it was not easy to change the immemorial habits of their race.

In the late summer of 1849 it began to rain. The cold, prolonged wet season that is usual in late fall came that year as early as August. Day after day the rain fell. At intervals there were torrents, saturating the hapless land. Tiny creeks usually gentle and limpid grew into angry, turgid rivers. The great rivers became wild floods that could not discharge their waters fast enough.

Garden plantings on fertile low spots were washed away. In the marshy sections the heads of the wild rice were far beneath the surface of the water. No vegetables or rice were harvested that year. Autumn was deepening into winter, with no help at hand. By 1849 the American Fur Company had closed many posts and had retrenched all along the line of its operations. The grand regime to which the Indians had adjusted themselves in two centuries was over.

In this dark situation, there was one ray of hope: the government payment, which was to be made unusually late that year.

[163]

There was still vague talk of moving the Indians westward. The treaty which finally settled that matter had not yet been made, but in order to encourage a voluntary migration, the annual payments were held just a little farther west each year. This year the payment was scheduled at Sandy Lake, a considerable distance west of Lake Superior.

Absence from the payment was a forfeiture, under the long-established rule. To Sandy Lake, then, went most of the Lake Superior Indians. Unwillingly they traveled into a country they did not like, making a late-season journey of hundreds of miles by water, portage and trail.

Father Baraga, sensing disaster, persuaded most of his Assinins Indians to remain at home.

The weather conditions at Sandy Lake proved to be excessively bad. Rain and snow alternated unceasingly. The stock of food on hand was negligible. There was no adequate shelter for the thousands who came expecting to remain only a few days. In the all-pervading wetness it was even difficult to keep fires going. Hungry, cold, wet, miserable, in an environment they distrusted, they waited. Then disease invaded the encampment. A virulent form of measles broke out. Children sickened and died. The poor food and the exposure brought dysentery. Within a few days more than two hundred were dead.

Still they waited. Surely the government had not forgotten them! Patience is a virtue of the Indian character. Day after miserable day they waited.

Then came a messenger: no payment would be made that year.

Wretched, dispirited, fearful, they fled the encampment. They left the sick on the spot to die; those that sickened during the flight homeward they left on the trail. Their canoes were waiting for them at the junction of the St. Louis and East Savan Rivers. When they came at last to that place, the St. Louis was frozen fast. Abandoning hundreds of the craft, they improvised snowshoes and fled homeward, demoralized and pitiable in their extremity.

Father Baraga was saddened to the very depths of his heart. He made no boast of his superior wisdom, though his own people whom he had persuaded to remain at home were infinitely better off, little as they had. That winter he traveled far and wide to reach the sufferers.

CHAPTER XXIII

FATHER BARAGA had once written in a letter to Europe: "Our Indians have the greatest desire to read, and they love their prayerbooks with passion. They take them along on their trips. At night when they go to bed they read and sing. I have seen some Indians who, on their deathbeds, requested as a last kindness that after death we put their prayerbooks on their breasts in their coffins."

It is not strange that in view of such a need the missionary had long since found time to produce writings in the Indian language. In his days at La Pointe, he had composed a Chippewa prayerbook and hymnal. It was at La Pointe also that he had written, for European publication, a short book on the life

[165]

and habits of the Lake Superior Indians, the modest proceeds of which were returned to him for use in his labors.

After establishing himself at L'Anse he began work on a comprehensive Chippewa dictionary and grammar. By 1853 it was ready for printing. He was eager to see it published because he believed it would help other priests who in the future would surely be engaged in Indian missionary work. In addition, there was now a pressing need for more copies of the prayerbook, which had originally been published in a very limited edition.

Under this compulsion, and also in the hope of getting another priest to help him, he decided late in the winter of 1853 to go to Cincinnati and make an appeal to the Archbishop for aid. He planned that his absence should fall while the Indians were at the annual maple-sugar-making so that he might be back at Assinins in season for the spring planting.

It is typical of the times that when he set forth, one day in March, he joined four other men in an impromptu traveling party. His companions were on their way to Milwaukee. Two of them had arrived from Ontonagon on snowshoes the day before and were going down to buy a lake vessel for copper cargoes. The other two, merchants from the Portage waterway, were bound for the city to get stocks of goods.

The route was southeasterly from L'Anse to Green Bay, a snowshoe journey of some two hundred miles. Green Bay was the northern terminus of a stage line that would take them south to the railroad. The overland trail was well marked, and afterward became the Military Road which joined Fort Howard on Green Bay with Fort Wilkins at Copper Harbor.

The party assembled three dog-trains at L'Anse to carry the luggage and provisions. By 1853 the dog-train was a common means of conveyance in the Lake Superior country. The train itself was virtually a toboggan about one foot wide and eight feet long. It was drawn over the snow by dogs harnessed in tandem. A cord attached to the tail of the train was used to guide the load and check it when going downhill. Since dogs could not travel far in deep snow, it was necessary that a trail be broken by men on snowshoes.

When the party reached the mouth of the Menominee River, the dog-trains were sent back to L'Anse with the two Indians who had charge of them. Horses and a sleigh were engaged from a settler to transport the missionary and his companions across Green Bay to the terminus of the stage line. They were proceeding over the bay ice when suddenly, at a drift of snow, the horses broke through. The travelers were thrown into the water, and for a time it seemed they must be lost; but the horses were able finally to scramble to firm ice again. Father Baraga's concern, once his companions were safe, was his manuscript, for the dictionary and grammar had taken years of work. Fortunately, after a great deal of effort all the baggage was retrieved. In frozen clothing the party completed the ice traverse. While they waited for the stage, they secured quarters in which to unpack and dry their things. With many a laughing comment his companions watched the priest separate his large manuscript, sheet by sheet, so that it would dry.

Father Baraga stopped at Milwaukee to pay his respects to Bishop Henni and then went on to Detroit where he visited his own Ordinary, Bishop Lefevre. He learned that a plan was on foot to erect a new ecclesiastical territory in the Lake Superior area. This new and growing territory, which was rapidly assuming an identity of its own, was at present part of three dioceses. The Indian missions constituted a special problem, scattered as they were about the Straits region and upon both shores

[167]

of Lake Superior. The Michigan missions had always been in the Detroit diocese, while those on the north shore of Lake Superior were in the Hamilton diocese of Canada. The Wisconsin missions had been detached from Detroit a few years previously and added to the Milwaukee diocese.

The new plan would separate the northern peninsula of Michigan, together with the mission stations in the Mackinac area, from the Detroit diocese; the Bishop of Hamilton would then cede the missions on the north shore of Lake Superior, and the Bishop of Milwaukee all of the western end of the lake. As in all such cases of new ecclesiastical divisions in missionary countries, the province would be known as a vicariate apostolic until its progress and development were assured, when it would become in actual fact a diocese.

Father Baraga found that both Bishop Henni and Bishop Lefevre desired the change. They stressed the point that Milwaukee and Detroit were rapidly growing cities, and that the Lake Superior country was too remote for them to give its problems the attention they required.

Following his visit in Detroit, Father Baraga went on to Cincinnati.

What with arranging to finance the printing of his new book and the new edition of the prayerbook, and working with the printers (there was no one else to assist them through the difficulties of Chippewa), he was occupied constantly. Weeks slipped by. Immersed in his publishing venture, which he could not leave until it was completed, he was nevertheless ceaselessly anxious about affairs at Assinins. He was preparing to return thither when he received word that Archbishop Purcell wished to confer with him.

It was apparent at once that the Archbishop was in a pleasant humor. He reviewed the plans for the new vicariate at some length. Rome had assented — the Vicariate Apostolic of Sault Ste. Marie and Marquette was now established. Who did Father Baraga think would make a good Bishop for it?

The missionary ventured to say that it would be a poor vicariate with a Bishop and but two priests!

The Archbishop laughed heartily. "Father Baraga," he said, "I have been teasing you a little. Now in all seriousness I make an announcement. I have letters from the Holy See. There has been created the Vicariate of Sault Ste. Marie and Marquette. Frederic Baraga has been appointed its first Bishop."

Father Baraga was overwhelmed. But it was not only surprise and gratitude that he felt. It was apprehension as well.

He could not, now, return to Lake Superior immediately. There was first his consecration, which was to be held in Cincinnati. Then there was the matter of priests to work in his territory. In conversations with the Archbishop it soon became evident that he could not hope to find these priests in America, where in many other quarters the need was as pressing as in his own field.

There was no alternative. He must await the ceremony of consecration and then proceed to Europe as quickly as possible.

He had time to ponder his problem. The Indian missions that now came under his jurisdiction had practically all been either established by him or served by him at one time or another. They stretched from the vicinity of Traverse Bay on Lake Michigan, through the Straits of Mackinac, up St. Mary's River to Sault Ste. Marie, and along both shores of Lake Superior. In that great territory there were now many new settlements which were no more than frontier villages. Others were of considerable antiquity, such as St. Ignace, Mackinac Island, Sault Ste. Marie and La Pointe. Potentially, there were great cities in the making, as at Duluth and Superior, past which he had gone many times on his way to Fond du Lac. There were the new towns of Marquette in the iron-mining district; Copper Harbor, Eagle Harbor and Eagle River on the Keweenaw peninsula, foreshadowing a greater copper country centering about Houghton, Hancock and Calumet; and Ontonagon, portal to another copper-mining district, Ashland, Port William, Fort Arthur.

Well, he knew that now he would have to begin calling upon the last reserves of his energy. The navigation season on Lake Superior is roughly the six months following mid-April. True, he could take the quite comfortable steamboats which now plied their routes on regular schedule. Nevertheless he knew that no office could save him the canoe voyages and the foot trails of that country — summer and winter.

On the feast of All Saints, 1853, in the cathedral at Cincinnati, Frederic Baraga was consecrated as titular Bishop of Amyzonia. There was unconscious irony in the fact that that title, redolent of the Mediterranean clime, now belonged to the chief shepherd of a land covered half the year with snow and ice. Not long after his consecration Bishop Baraga sailed for Europe.

CHAPTER XXIV

BISHOP BARAGA was celebrating Mass in the cathedral at Laibach. The last time he had offered Mass here he was twenty-six years old; now he was fifty-seven.

Attending, Amalia watched him. That devout and devoted sister, now his only living relative, may be forgiven her absorption in the brother she had not seen for so many years.

He looks so old, she was thinking; and, dear God, he is so frail! She studied his head and his face. The fair brown hair that she remembered, still worn long, was thinner, and its luster had been bleached away by sun and wind. The fine features were drawn in deep-etched lines that spoke of self-denial and physical suffering. His skin was tanned as dark as that of one of his Indians.

But Amalia was aware of an exaltation in the great crowd of people jamming the cathedral. She divined that this, to them, was an extraordinary experience. Every eye was upon the American Bishop. Slowly his sister began to understand. There is a change in him, she thought, there is something which was not there before. He had achieved, through the long years of devotion to his mission in the wilderness, both great nobility and great humility, and this strange concomitance marked him as one set apart from the crowd. And yet to Amalia these were not new characteristics. She remembered them in his youth. Nevertheless, his experience in the new world had sublimated them, and in the blending a single impression was given the observer: utter simplicity, so sincere that it was astonishing. It made itself felt now to the great congregation, and Amalia herself was a little breathless as realization came to her.

[171]

The sister, who up to that moment had cherished a certain measure of pride, felt now as though her brother had looked with his mild blue eyes straight into her heart. She was ashamed of what he might have seen, and returned to her prayers in a little rush of humility.

Dear God, this is not Frederic Baraga, the small brother whom I mothered, she thought. He is not even the young priest whom I saw celebrate Mass at this very altar. Dear God, You have set some holy light to shine upon him!

Yet neither the Bishop nor Amalia was fully sensible of the feeling of the people in the countryside around the old Baraga home. For they found a kind of consecration of themselves in the crozier and miter of the American prelate. It was something that lifted them above themselves, something that made grace and goodness more real to them. This little Illyria had given him to the service of God; in raising him so high, God had done heavenly honor to them.

In Vienna, whither he had gone to appeal to the Leopoldine Society for funds to help sustain his work in a yet unorganized diocese, Bishop Baraga was invited as one of many prelates to the wedding of Emperor Franz Joseph of Austria and Princess Elizabeth of Bavaria. At the reception in the royal palace, among the ornate and lavish furnishings and the fashionable and extravagant court costumes, he was ill at ease. I have become an American, he told himself, and not realized it before. His unique position as an American Bishop who lived with the Indians in the wilderness singled him out for general interest. But the sumptuous feast, the gay and shallow talk, irked him. The scene called up, by contrast, the grim realities of life on Lake Superior. I am not part of this, the missionary thought. I was born to it and now I am intolerant of it. I yearn to return to the poverty of my people in America.

He was aware of some movement of the guests, and a chamberlain requested him to take his place in the line that was forming by some scheme of rank written on a paper in the court official's hand. Thus he arrived before the emperor. A functionary read his name, stating his rank together with other brief data. He did not listen. He took the gem-incrusted gifts that were placed in his hands, acknowledged them with a bow and passed on.

He accepted the invitation of King Ferdinand of Bavaria and went to Prague, and again in line at the king's reception he received rich gifts.

Bishop Baraga stood in the room of a gem merchant in a little street in Rome. In a short while he would go on to the Vatican to have an audience with the Pope. He felt again in his pockets to make sure that the copies of his Chippewa prayer-book and Chippewa dictionary were there. They were to be presented to the Holy Father.

On the table before him lay the gifts of king and emperor. The merchant was appraising them with an expert eye. Again they were placed in the counterweighted scale on the table, one at a time. Again the gems were examined, each by itself, through a magnifying glass. At the same time the merchant was appraising his customer. He was just a little confused by the rapid impressions running through his mind. The clerical garb, the deep eyes bent upon him, disturbed his calculations.

Italian? Certainly not. French? Spanish?

"Your country, my lord?"

"I am an American missionary."

The merchant turned this and many other matters over in his thoughts, mingling them in a quick computation. At last with many protestations and explanations he named a price.

The Bishop was a little impatient.

"Sir, I do not know the value of these articles. I came to you upon the recommendation of a Monsignor who knows you. You will do well not to cheat me, and you will pay me only what these articles are worth."

The merchant looked up into the mild blue eyes. He decided to say that, because of this and that condition in the market, he could pay something more than the amount of his first offer.

Bishop Baraga accepted the money, turned his back upon the rich gifts that still lay on the table, and walked into the street. He had no compunctions. He appreciated the gifts. He had no mind to criticize a social order that now seemed strange to him. It was only that he knew what he wanted, he knew where he belonged. As he walked up the little street, nostalgia for Lake Superior seized and held him.

The Vicar Apostolic of Sault Ste. Marie and Marquette sat in a room at St. Sulpice's in Paris, waiting. He was here because he knew that this school above all others was famous as a trainer of priests for foreign missions. The school officials had announced his presence to the entire student body, explaining his desire to interview any who were willing to go to his vicariate in America.

There were many. Each presented himself carrying a written record of the essential facts about him. The Bishop questioned them little, encouraged them to talk. While they talked,

On the table before them lay the gifts of king and emperor.

[175]

he studied them. He was looking for inner forces, for the marks of spiritual stature: he was looking for potential apostles. He realized that none of these candidates knew the conditions under which he would be working in America. But the Bishop knew. He rejected all but one of them.

Young Martin Fox talked less than any of the others. Yet Bishop Baraga saw in him what he was looking for. He could envision Martin Fox on Lake Superior — sure, serene, able, strong, willing. The young man knew only French and German, so the Bishop arranged that he should attend All Hallows in Dublin for a year, devoting himself to the mastery of English. At the end of that time he was to report for duty at Sault Ste. Marie.

Waiting for a ship, Bishop Baraga reviewed the results of his sojourn in Europe. He had had an audience with the Pope. He had received assurance of sustained assistance from the Leopoldine Society. He had seen his boyhood home and visited Amalia. From the sale of the royal presents he had acquired some cash for the more urgent immediate needs of his poor missions. He had found Martin Fox. He had arranged with other Bishops for the release to him of such older priests as were willing to come to Lake Superior.

But he was thinking of all that remained to be done, as he sailed for home.

CHAPTER XXV

SAULT STE. MARIE, seat of the vicariate, was a small, unattractive village in 1854. Yet it was old, as antiquity is measured in America. It had been the site of an Indian village from time unknown, and as early as 1668 Father Marquette had established a mission station there. Situated on the St. Mary's waterway at the great rapids, it was the portal to Lake Superior. Over the sault the waters of the immense lake tumble frenziedly to reach the lower lakes.

The isolation of Lake Superior for nearly two centuries is evidenced by the size and condition of this portal during all that time. When the copper rush destroyed the isolation, Sault Ste. Marie numbered perhaps two hundred inhabitants. It had been no larger in the greatest days of the fur trade in spite of the fact that it was used by the Northwest Company, the Hudson Bay Company and the American Fur Company. Through the tiny settlement passed all the traffic to the north and northwest in an import-export trade that involved uncounted millions of dollars' worth of furs and merchandise. Yet even in 1820 Sault Ste. Marie boasted less than a score of permanent dwellings. In the high tide of the copper rush itself, there were not more than perhaps fifty buildings in the town.

But its importance must be gauged, not by the number of its buildings, but by its situation. It was a place where men must stop, if only briefly, between destinations unrelated to the spot itself.

Jean Nicolet, in 1634, paused at the portal and named the falls of the river "Rapids of Gaston," though the appellation never came into general use. In 1641, Charles Raymbault and Isaac Jogues gave river and falls the name of "St. Mary's." Ménard passed through in 1660, to enter Lake Superior and then to disappear at L'Anse. Radisson and his companion, Groseilliers, stopped there on the journey that led to the organization of the Hudson Bay Company.

In all those years, the first white man who made any attempt to establish a settlement was Father Marquette, in 1668. Even so, it was 1671 before St.-Lusson came to assume formal possession in the name of France. But Sault Ste. Marie was still a portal when it was taken by the British and a portal it remained for some time in the hands of the United States.

Perhaps all the time that we have been using the word "portal" we should have used the word "stile." Lake Superior is higher than the other lakes and much of the difference in elevation is traversed within a distance of a few hundred feet in the leap or "sault" of St. Mary's River. At the foot of this charging water was the village of Sault Ste. Marie, or as was the usage for two centuries, Sault de Ste. Marie. Water travel was checked by these rapids — white torrents rushing and tumbling as though all the mighty pressure of Lake Superior was driving them. Travelers stopped at the village and prepared for a portage or "carry." That was a simple matter with canoes, and the distance was not great. But if you had a large lake vessel carrying cargo, the impediment was serious. All you could do was transfer the cargo by land around the falls from one vessel to another — a laborious and expensive operation.

For some years after Father Baraga settled at La Pointe, all the shipping on Lake Superior was handled by the American Fur Company's "John Jacob Astor." Subsequently other vessels appeared, built below the rapids and moved around them —

inched along on rollers in the manner of house-moving — to be launched above. Obviously, the size of these boats was limited by the necessity of moving them on land.

But now there was developing on Lake Superior shipping tonnage in terms of millions of tons. The handling of heavy cargoes was prohibitive in cost. For some years, it is true, the copper cargoes were transferred by portage from one vessel to another; but copper was shipped compactly, often in barrels. Iron was an altogether different matter. The ore was taken from the mines in a loose mass similar to sand or gravel. It was out of the question to handle such bulky cargo twice.

The accomplishment of the engineering feat that circumvented the rapids to make one continuous water passage coincided almost exactly with the establishment by Bishop Baraga of the seat of his vicariate at Sault Ste. Marie. When he arrived there in August, 1854, work had been going on for a year or more. The locks and canal were opened in 1855. What happened then is the astounding history of the growth of an inland empire which emptied its products through that portal to create a commercial traffic exceeding the wildest dreams of even the most optimistic of the pioneers who began the Lake Superior exploitation. From that beginning the canal and locks had to be enlarged again and again.

Bishop Baraga's Sault Ste. Marie, small as it was before the building of the canal, had a distinction that made it quite different from any other town in his territory. Fort Brady squatted on the bank of the river and the little settlement huddled about it.

The flavor of the place was distinctly French, even to the narrow streets that gave access to the small buildings. Perhaps there were five hundred permanent inhabitants when the Bishop

arrived. Many Indians, not so migratory as elsewhere, lived in
the close vicinity. The garrison at the fort did not exceed fifty
officers and men. Most of the dwellings were low log struc-
tures. There was not a real residence in the place. The "cathedral" was not as good an edifice as the church he had built at
La Pointe.

During the navigation season, of course, there was great
activity at the water front. Vessels from lower lake ports such
as Buffalo, Cleveland and Detroit tied up at the docks below
the rapids and discharged cargoes consigned to the mines on
Lake Superior. A tram road for little cars drawn by horses
ran from these docks to the docks above the rapids where the
goods were reloaded on lake vessels. But in winter Sault Ste.
Marie became again its ancient, sleepy self. The character of
the settlement's inhabitants gave winter life a kind of gay
charm. The French Canadians were a hospitable, happy people
given to the enjoyment of festivity. Fiddling and dancing were
common. For all of the impending changes, in winter the traditions of the place were fur-trade traditions. Few lived there as
yet whose ancestors had not been part of that colorful and romantic regime. The voyageur had not quite passed out of the
picture. But revolution had arrived. The Canadian of the fur-
trade days worked hard through the winter and loafed in summer; now he worked hard all summer and loafed through the
winter.

Those who live through momentous changes do not usually
recognize what is happening. But with the canal opened to the
passage of ships, Bishop Baraga wrote in his journal: "The
future fills me with uneasiness."

American surveyors running their lines for the construction
of the canal came upon a great, moss-incrusted cedar cross par-

tially fallen from its base and half-buried in the litter of under-brush. It was the cross planted by St.-Lusson when that cavalier took possession of the site in the name of the Bourbons. Now the engineers threw it aside and forgot it. When the lines of the canal were laid and shovels were struck into the ground to dig the excavation, the builders unearthed an ancient Indian burial ground. Learning of these things, Bishop Baraga thought: The lilies of the Bourbons withered here. The bones of an ancient race are crumbled and forgotten. There is nothing eternal about man on earth, nor about the work of his hands. These are ashes and dust. Yet here in this earth was perhaps the body of one whom Marquette instructed in the way of eternal life.

But there was no time for contemplation in the face of pressing duties. Reaching Sault Ste. Marie on August 20, he was a passenger on a steamer bound for La Pointe five days later. At La Pointe he confirmed almost a hundred. The following day he went to Ontonagon where on September 8 he confirmed twenty. By September 18 he was back at Sault Ste. Marie, but in three days had taken steamer for L'Anse, where on October 1 he confirmed forty-three at Assinins. Again at the Sault, he celebrated there on October 12 his first Pontifical High Mass in his diocese, and confirmed eighty-five. On October 28 he went to Payment on St. Mary's River to confirm forty-three. Then he left for Mackinac where he remained until after Easter, making several trips to settlements about the Straits. In late April he proceeded to Detroit and thence to Cincinnati, to take up the problem of his printing once more. On June 24 he was finally back at Sault Ste. Marie.

Thus in the ten months following his arrival he had journeyed up Lake Superior twice, had organized his work throughout the Straits region, and had made a sojourn at Cincinnati.

[181]

Sault Ste. Marie had seen little of him. Nor did it see more now. By July 9 he was again on Lake Superior visiting Marquette, Eagle River, Eagle Harbor, L'Anse, La Pointe and Ontonagon. He returned to the Sault early in September. In the first year of his episcopacy he journeyed, by the poor accommodations of that time, many thousands of miles. Of the twelve months he probably spent less than one at Sault Ste. Marie. Here, apparently, was a Bishop who meant to see his people face to face down to the least and the poorest in the farthest corner of a far-flung diocese. What of a residence, an office and a cathedral? Those must wait.

CHAPTER XXVI

THE Bishop had had no experience as an administrator. His whole mature life had been spent in undertakings the success or failure of which depended solely on his personal attention to details. There was not, could not be, any impersonality in anything Frederic Baraga attempted. The La Pointe and L'Anse missions were so much a part of him that they had a character wholly different than they would have had if built by another.

Yet the very lack of administrative experience was an advantage in the early circumstances of his episcopal work. There were places which no priest could be found to serve and in these places the Bishop himself performed the duties of Indian missionary or parish priest as the conditions required. He had no lordly ideas. He could not be changed by a title. His cathedral itself was a small parish church at which for some time he had not even an assistant. He was moving about in a vicariate that was as yet merely a name.

This was no new condition. Indeed, the principal reasons for the establishment of the new ecclesiastical province were to correct the deficiency of priests in a territory where they were badly needed, and then to bring administration closer to the area to be governed.

For twenty years, except during short sojourns in Detroit and Cincinnati, Bishop Baraga had rarely seen another priest. For twenty years he himself had been the parish priest of Lake Superior. The quality of his devotion and the degree of his sacrifice could not be taken as norms even in a field where self-lessness was the rule. The zeal of his ministry was altogether extraordinary. But this was not so evident to him as it was to others. And now, inexperienced as he was in judging other priests, understanding as he did the needs of his vicariate better than his co-workers in it, it was nevertheless immediately in-cumbent on him to select men with some previous seminary education, continue their training privately, and ordain them.

So the Bishop began with the first men who came to him. Some were recruited through Bishops in Europe, others were sent to him from American sources where his pressing needs were known.

From minor orders to subdeaconship, to deaconship, and finally to priesthood, the candidate's advancement is correlated with an orderly progression in study. But when you have no priest at all and you badly need several score, too rigid tests of attainment are impossible. How quickly the process was car-ried through under the pressure of need is shown in the case of

Father Henry Thiele, Bishop Baraga's first candidate. The Bishop found the young man waiting for him at the Sault when he returned from his first trip up Lake Superior in 1854. On September 20 he raised the candidate to minor orders, on October 11 to the subdiaconate, one week later to the diaconate. On October 21 the Bishop ordained him priest. By November 3 Father Thiele was on his way to the parish at Eagle Harbor. He was the first of several so ordained.

Not all of the early priests in the vicariate were ordained by Bishop Baraga. Gradually, a few older, experienced priests came. In December of 1854 Father Duroc met the Bishop at Mackinac Island and was immediately assigned to St. Ignace. Father Jahan was established at Mackinac Island.

There came to the Bishop at the Sault in this early, anxious time young Edward Jacker. Given minor orders in July, 1855, he was ordained on August 5 and immediately assigned to L'Anse. As we shall see, the time came when Father Jacker was truly a right arm to his enfeebled Bishop.

Father Van Paemel went to La Pointe. Martin Fox, arrived from his studies in Dublin, was within a month of his arrival an ordained priest, and on his way to Ontonagon. Father Benoit was ordained and sent to Port William on the north shore.

Port William, Grand Portage, Superior, La Pointe; Ontonagon with its neighboring mine settlements at Rockland, Norwich and Greenland; Eagle River and the interior mining locations; Eagle Harbor, Copper Harbor, L'Anse, Marquette, Sault Ste. Marie; St. Ignace, Mackinac Island, the missions on Traverse Bay and at Manistique: it was a tremendous province crying out its needs to its Bishop, pressing him for priests, demanding his personal presence.

[184]

Though happiest with his Indians, he was compelled to give most of his attention to the growing, turbulent towns. Not all of the priests he had ordained proved worthy of the confidence he placed in them. Let them go unnamed. Problems crowded thick about him. Exhausted and aging, he sat in his bare room at the Sault one November night in 1856 and wrote in his journal: "Today is the third anniversary of my consecration. A very sad day. I would almost say: Let that day be turned into darkness. Let darkness and the shadow of death cover it, let a mist overspread it, and let it be wrapped up in bitterness." Thus he cried out with Job. Nor was this the end of his desolation. Two years later on that anniversary he confided to his journal: "The past saddens me; the present torments me; the future frightens me. I would infinitely prefer to be an Indian missionary."

At his return from Europe, Ontonagon had become the largest town on Lake Superior. The metropolis of that rampant, raw and self-conscious thing known as the copper boom, it was not itself a mining town, but the result of the development of one very rich and many promising copper mines a few miles inland. These mines used the river for transportation; their supplies were unloaded from lake vessels in Ontonagon, at the mouth of the river, and their copper was shipped from the Ontonagon harbor. It was a busy harbor, lined with docks and warehouses, in a town of boarding houses, hotels and saloons.

Notwithstanding the size and importance of the place, it had no church. Worse — as Ontonagon was the largest of the towns built by the copper rush, it furnished in abundance all the undesirable elements of the new type of civilization that had come upon Lake Superior. The Bishop had no need to acquaint himself with the place, at least as far as the Indians were concerned. He knew every Ontonagon Indian by name. But now, in spite of all his efforts to persuade them to leave, the Indians stubbornly remained in that environment. What had happened to them may well be imagined. Whiskey was the commonest article of trade. All of the missionary's years of work with them seemed destined to be lost.

"Ah, misère!" groaned Bishop Baraga to his journal. "I am at Ontonagon waiting for a boat."

But he came in the fall of 1854 to establish a parish and erect a church.

On every visit to Ontonagon, he had inveighed with all his zeal against the liquor traffic with the Indians. He was horrified at its consequences. Now the witless host of a public hostelry at which he was compelled to stay, attempted to embarrass him. Probably the incident could have happened nowhere else and at no other time. It is a part of the half-madness of the copper boom.

The man ordered a cake made with brandy to be served to Bishop Baraga for his dinner. The missionary ate unquestioningly. When he had finished his meal, the gloating host came forward, rubbing his hands and smiling a satisfied smile.

"Bishop Baraga," he began, "you have often objected to our selling liquor to the Indians, and you have often told them that you yourself never touch it. Isn't that true?"

· "That is true," the Bishop replied.

"Did you like the cake, Bishop? I thought you seemed to relish it."

"The cake was excellent," Bishop Baraga told him.

"Ah," exclaimed the grinning host, "don't you think a preacher should practice what he preaches?"

"Most certainly."

"Well, Bishop, you have just eaten cake with brandy in it!" The man cackled with laughter.

Bishop Baraga could scarcely believe that he had heard aright. He looked searchingly into the man's face for a long moment. When he spoke his voice was soft and gentle.

"I am very sorry for you," he told the landlord.

On this trip Bishop Baraga remained at Ontonagon for two weeks. He administered Confirmation and dedicated the new church to St. Patrick. He had brought with him a young priest whom he had ordained and who was to be left in charge of the Ontonagon parish — the predecessor of Father Martin Fox.

Now the Bishop felt that he had made a little progress. The Indians promised better behavior. The number of parishioners was gratifying. Some dissension among them had been smoothed away. It was a fair hope that St. Patrick's might become in time one of the strongest stations of his territory.

Stopping for several days at L'Anse on his way back to the Sault, he found difficulties that detained him longer than he had planned. Since he had as yet no priest who could speak the Chippewa language well, it was necessary for him to give certain matters his personal attention. When he finally arrived at Sault Ste. Marie he was astonished to find there the young priest he had left at Ontonagon to serve the parish. From the runaway's story it was soon apparent that he lacked the stuff to meet the problems of missionary life on Lake Superior. The Bishop had believed in this man, had instructed him with care and diligence. Now he was a failure — a failure in his first test! The excuses he offered for leaving his post were flimsy and the Bishop brushed them aside. It was one of the few times that he

[187]

lost patience. Without ceremony, he dismissed the young priest from service in the vicariate.

Nevertheless, he laid much of the fault upon himself. The incident depressed him. He had misconceived the priest's character. Might he not fall into the same error again? He chided himself. Why had he not recognized the weakness of this young man? He feared irreparable damage had resulted. At home only a day, he hurried back to Ontonagon to attempt to undo what he felt his own bad judgment had wrought.

If it was his fault, he corrected it amply. The time came when he looked with great pride upon this Ontonagon parish, for it grew rapidly and finally supported an Ursuline convent and school, the only one in his territory. And he had, too, the satisfaction of placing Father Martin Fox at the head of the parish.

While he was at the western end of Lake Superior in the autumn of 1854, an event occurred that was to have a marked effect on the future of his Indian missions. The long-argued question of the Indian removal was settled.

No one knew better than Bishop Baraga the discontent among the Chippewas over matters that grew out of their own credulousness when making treaties. Never, it seemed, did the white and the Indian mind really meet. When the government proceeded to exercise its rights under prior treaties, the Indians were always astounded to discover the consequences of their own act in signing these binding obligations.

The missionary had seen Buffalo depart from La Pointe in 1837 to go to St. Peter on the upper Mississippi where the treaty of that year was made. Afterward Buffalo explained carefully to him what he had understood the agreement to be.

"We were told," Buffalo related, "that our Great White Father in Washington wants the large pine trees and the minerals in the rocks. He does not want the land for he thinks it is too cold in this country to make farms. We were told that the Great White Father does not want the trees that the Indians use. He does not want the maple that gives us our sugar. He does not want the birch and cedar that make our canoes and lodges. We do not use the large pine trees and we do not care if he takes them. We do not care if he takes the minerals in the rocks. Our white brothers will make kettles and implements which they will trade to us for fish and fur. All that is good. We agreed to that and we signed the paper."

Bishop Baraga saw the treaty of 1842 negotiated at La Pointe. In the long ceremonial speeches, the Indians' minds were still fixed on the big pine trees and the minerals in the rocks, while the single thing in the mind of the government representative was to persuade the Indians to cede their title to the land itself. The Indian mind was not quite capable of grasping that idea, and the chiefs wandered far afield in their speeches; they were mainly interested in an agreement that the annual government payment be made at La Pointe and at no other place for twenty-five years. Pressed on the subject of title transfer, they said, "It is not the land but what is on the land that matters. We gave you what you asked for at St. Peter in 1837. You are welcome to take the things you asked for and which we gave you." Nevertheless, when the paper was signed, the Indian title to the land had been ceded.

As time went on it became increasingly evident that the Indians supposed they had a right, even under the terms of the La Pointe treaty, to wander upon and use any and all of the lands at will. It seemed impossible for them to comprehend the offense of trespass. Thus the agitation for moving them westward, off the lands to which they had ceded title, was never understood by the Indians. The truth is that by that time the fur companies were not without guile in promoting such agitation; the traders had moved their posts westward and they wanted the Indians to follow them.

The government did not wish to resort to compulsory migration. This situation led up to the treaty of 1854, whereby the Indians were forced to accept the government's concept of land ownership although they did not yet understand it. They were told that they had one of two choices. Either they could move westward, or the government would give them back certain restricted portions of land, which they might choose themselves but upon which they must stay. These chosen sites were to be called reservations. This latter plan the Indians accepted. They selected the sites and the treaty was signed.

Bishop Baraga was elated to learn that one of the places on which choice fell was L'Anse. Many Indians would now be required to go there and remain. Moreover, the government was obligated to safeguard their rights and to punish invaders — the lawless white man must keep out. Finally, the long-disputed question of moving the Chippewas westward was settled at last.

The other sites chosen under the treaty were wisely chosen for the most part. The missionary was now free to make definite plans for his Indian mission stations.

A great deal of reserve energy had been expended on the last trip up the lake, and back at Sault Ste. Marie, he was tired and unwell. Indigestion had enfeebled him. He had a temporary spell of marked deafness. A slight involuntary shaking

of his head and his hands came upon him with increasing fre-
quency. But to balance these things he had also news of cheer.

Some months before, he had received letters telling him
that Father Chebul, a priest from the vicinity of his old home
in Illyria, had decided to come to his vicariate in America. All
of the letters spoke highly of Father Chebul's attainments and
zeal. Bishop Baraga was greatly pleased to know that his trip
to Europe had been thus fruitful. Now he would have the services of a priest who was still young but who had already gained
experience and attracted the attention of his superiors.

A vessel coming up the river from the lower lakes was
bringing the new missionary. The moment the plank was
lowered the Bishop mounted it to the deck. He saw Father
Chebul standing alone and rushed up to him, greeting him
warmly. At Father Chebul's feet were two enormous sachels.
These the Bishop immediately seized.

"Oh, no!" Father Chebul cried, seeing the Bishop's intention. "I will carry the luggage!" And he tried to retrieve the
burden.

"Never mind, come along," Bishop Baraga told him, leading the way off the boat.

"No, no!" the priest remonstrated. "You must give me the
satchels. What will people say when they see my Bishop carrying my luggage!" He tried again to get hold of the satchels.

Bishop Baraga stopped and looked at him. "I will carry
them," he said firmly. Then, after a moment, he added as
though in explanation, "I am old and used to these things. You
have much work to do and you must spare yourself."

Strange America! thought Father Chebul as he followed his
Bishop along the dock. A dozen or so men greeted Bishop
Baraga with marked deference as his slight figure hurried along

[191]

the wharf sagging under the weight of the luggage, but none of them offered to relieve him. Father Chebul was to learn.

They went up Lake Superior next day to La Pointe, where the newcomer was to be stationed. When they arrived at their sleeping quarters in the town, the accommodation proved to be one narrow bed. The Bishop directed Father Chebul to occupy it.

"But where will you sleep?" asked the priest.

"I shall be very comfortable for I am used to this and you are not." And Bishop Baraga began to make up a pallet on the floor.

Father Chebul would not permit such a thing — if he could stop it. "I would not sleep all night for thinking of my Bishop on the floor!" he pleaded.

Now the Bishop's tone was a little sharp.

"You will occupy the bed. I have spent hundreds of nights in poorer places. I am used to these things. I am old and it does not matter. You are young and must spare yourself — "

"No! I cannot consider — "

"You will occupy the bed! I am your Bishop and it is your duty to obey me!"

CHAPTER XXVII

IN 1856, three years after it was founded, the Vicariate Apostolic of Sault Ste. Marie and Marquette was raised to the rank of a diocese and Bishop Baraga was given the title of Bishop of Sault Ste. Marie.

This was not now the Frederic Baraga who had first come to Lake Superior in 1835. The vision and resolve of the old La Pointe days were still there, but a quarter of a century of missionary life in a rigorous climate had taken its toll. Yet, if that life had taken something away, it had given something also. Unconsciously, from long, close contact with the Indians, he had learned to assume their outward stoical calm. The perplexities, the myriad trials of his office were grappled with inwardly, and if failure was the outcome of any project, he blamed no one except himself. His journal reveals much about those inner struggles, that at times almost overwhelmed him as age and sickness gradually sapped the strength of his body.

Often now a thick and enveloping veil of melancholy settled upon him. He could penetrate it, emerge from it, only through a desperate energy for work. At these times, the return to primitive modes of travel gave him complete satisfaction. In a canoe with his Indians he could forget for long hours the heavy load that the office of Bishop placed on his shoulders. The canoe floating under a serene blue sky soothed and comforted him. The acrid smoke of the little wood fires when they stopped to make camp, brought to him pleasant memories of almost forgotten experiences. He was missionary to the Indians again, sitting at their camp fires. The Indian words were pleasant in his ears. Every point of land, every bay and cove was a familiar landmark to him. He could close his eyes and even those experiences that had been cruel at the time were softened and mellowed in retrospect. He floated again beneath the streaming banners of the Northern Lights, and the *chanson* of the voyageur came soft and nostalgic over the water. In these summer months, for long idyllic hours as he traveled far off the steamer lanes, he lived in the past and found it pleasant.

[193]

Occasionally, however, he was overwhelmed by a sense of its loss: something good was gone and could never be regained. Now I am a Bishop, he thought. Is it possible that I really built my first church at La Pointe a quarter of a century ago? But at La Pointe the old familiar scene was disappearing and he could recreate it only in his mind. Many of those great axemen who had built the little church of St. Joseph in love and sweat were in their graves, and he was now confirming their grandchildren.

Consciously he set his feet on old trails and sat alone on familiar beaches. In spirit he talked again with Douglass Houghton of the empire that was coming into being. He sat in old lodges — now there were so many in his memory, they were almost countless.

From these reminiscences he would arouse suddenly, thinking that too much of his life was behind him.

Early one morning at the Sault, during a very severe cold spell, his assistant told him that an Indian had come in the night asking that the Bishop return with him to a dying brother a long distance from the poor episcopal residence.

"You were asleep and did not hear our caller," the young priest explained. "I told him you were not well and could not be disturbed. He should have known that it is too cold and the distance is too far for you to go in the nighttime. I offered to go back with him but he wanted only you."

"Who is this man and where is he now?" demanded the Bishop.

Naming the Indian, the assistant replied that the man had returned home alone.

Bishop Baraga sprang to his feet and hurriedly assembled a pack. The assistant sought to restrain him, reminding him again of his recent illness, only to be chided for not having aroused him as soon as the Indian came. Not even waiting for breakfast, the Bishop called the two Indian boys who were living with him that winter and laid out their lessons for the day, with hasty admonitions. Then, just at daylight, he slipped into the half-running gait that he had learned would take him fast and far on snowshoes. All his diocese might wait until he had consummated this journey of mercy.

Thus the years went by. As troubles arose in the parishes, the only solution he had was an unconscious division of one bishop into many parish priests. It is not to the point to say he was not a good administrator. These were troubles that no amount of administrative ability could have obviated. They lay deep in the defective character of the men who caused them, deep in racial hatreds, deep in the circumstances that had cast these people upon these shores in the flood that was the expansion of America.

Only Bishop Baraga could resolve them. Only Bishop Baraga's physical presence could allay them.

"My dearly beloved children in Christ. . . ."

The depth of spirituality, the quiet, simple dignity, the sound of the gentle voice that betokened complete sincerity, made them ashamed of their little meannesses. They were children indeed sitting before a father whose heart throbbed with love for them.

But he could not be omnipresent. The diocese was molding itself and building itself, in a physical sense, into a rich and distinctive part of a great nation. Old and sensitive traditions were being uprooted and trampled upon by the new order. Up and down the great diocese the Bishop traveled. He was known everywhere, even by the newest comer. His personal acquaintance was universal — rich and poor, Catholic and Protestant, Indian and white.

Trouble at Ontonagon — would it never cease?

For the second time, Frederic Baraga's life was threatened.

The affairs of the Ontonagon parish were in turmoil, different nationalities having formed themselves into angry factions. It became necessary for the Bishop to state with finality his position in the inciting controversy. By the time of his arrival the contending elements had lost all sense of responsibility. The parishioners were a mob milling about the church. There had been physical clashes and the peace officers seemed powerless.

Into the midst of this frenzy stepped the frail old Bishop. Angry men circled around him — stopped and listened. He spoke directly, plainly. There was nothing now in what he said to beguile or soothe. There was no compromise.

Suddenly, as the import of his words reached the people, an infuriated man rushed up with the intent to strike the speaker down. Bishop Baraga stood quietly, without the slightest gesture of defense. Over the feeble old man towered his assailant, a huge stone clutched in his raised fist. Something in the quiet poise of the slight figure, something in the Bishop's countenance, held the angry man's arm aloft. Breathlessly the crowd saw that moment of indecision, watched the arm slowly descend and the threatener walk away.

In the afternoon an accident occurred at Ontonagon among a crew of men engaged in some heavy work. In the accident the arm that had been lifted against Bishop Baraga was shorn from its shoulder.

That autumn at the Sault his sense of failure seemed immitigable. Self-abasement swept him, wave over wave. The years of his life rolled off before him, and between the few moments of great drama were the endless, monotonous days when he had set one foot before the other on a hundred trails with dogged perseverance. He felt caught and enslaved in futility, in frustration.

Fortunately no man is capable of self-measurement. He had written in his journal this year: "My fifth anniversary. Sad. The past saddens me; the present torments me; the future frightens me." The past saddened him because he believed he had missed the fulness of the opportunity to consummate a successful mission; he had no regrets except the regret of a golden chance he imagined lost. As for the present, undoubtedly it tormented him with its incessant vexing problems. He considered seriously the idea of resigning his office.* He told himself over and over again that he was not fit to be a Bishop. Whatever had been his case before, it is certain that he had now come to the last station on the road of humility. And because no man is capable of self-measurement, he was never to realize that his profound humility was actually an innate force. For now it may be seen that at the very moment of seeming despair he was responding to the requirements of his office with spiritual greatness. Out of his very feebleness emanated a power so immeasurable that its influence still grows.

---

*Verwyst, p. 286, quotes the Baraga journal: "Dec. 15, 1856 — yesterday and today I have again thoughts of resigning."

The Straits had become a great fishery and Mackinaw trout was famous in the commercial markets of the nation. Hence, the men about the Straits country, who did most of the fishing, were away from home much of the time that the waters were open. Their homes were chiefly at Mackinac Island and St. Ignace, and accordingly the Bishop visited that part of his diocese during the winter months to be sure of finding his people there.

In January of 1860 he set off afoot for the Straits. As a compromise with necessity, he had engaged two stalwart half-breeds to accompany him. The snow was new and fluffy so that snowshoes sank deep, rendering the going difficult and progress slow.

Preceding the Bishop on the sixty-mile trail, his companions checked their pace so that they would not leave him too far behind. Two men will break a trail of considerable compactness, and along such a trail Bishop Baraga followed with labored effort. His feebleness was marked, and he shook with palsy.

The temperature was below zero, yet the exertion of each agonized mile brought out the sweat upon him. He could not continue long without a rest. He set one foot ahead of the other as though he were counting his steps. Every fiber of his body felt the strain. His breathing was constricted, and hot darts shot through his chest. His companions watched him, their hearts filled with compassion. Yet well they knew that they were expected to act as though nothing unusual were happening.

One night the party slept in an abandoned and dilapidated Indian lodge. Another night they made camp behind a wind-fallen tree, shoveling the snow away with their snowshoes, building a fire and arranging a bed of balsam boughs. Their fare was bread and tea. At both encampments the Bishop rose at four in the morning for his usual hours of prayer, his companions sleeping soundly in their blankets beside him.

At last they came out upon the ice of St. Martin's Bay, to the north of St. Ignace. Suddenly the man in the lead shouted and pointed. On the horizon was a fast-moving dark line coming straight toward them. As the distance lessened they made out several horse-drawn sleighs. Then they saw that each sleigh was gaily decorated, and now the sleigh bells shook silver notes into the frosty air. The people of St. Ignace had sent a guard of honor to meet their Bishop.

Within the wide circle into which the procession had swung, they knelt on the ice to receive his blessing. Then, comprehending something of his exhaustion, they showed their eager solicitude. Food, kept warm on heated stones under thick coverings in the sleighs, was brought forth. Finally, warmly wrapped, the Bishop was given the seat of honor at the head of the procession as they sped back to St. Ignace.

Upon their approach to the town, the church bell rang out with lively tempo and all the inhabitants of the little settlement came down to meet them, singing and rejoicing. They did not see a palsied old man; they saw only their strong, beloved shepherd and friend. His smile lit festive candles in their hearts, giving warmth and light.

Moments such as this were counterweights against the hours of self-questioning and despondency.

The following summer, the Bishop and Father Chebul were passengers on one of the lake steamers. Captain McKay, long on Lake Superior, had often carried the Bishop up and down his route. Gruffness of manner was a tradition among these lake captains, and Captain McKay ranked high in the fraternity in this respect. He could bellow orders with the best of them.

The dining saloon on Captain McKay's ship had one long table down the center, and as was the custom for the masters of the passenger boats, he occupied its head at mealtimes. On this occasion Father Chebul sat with the Bishop on one side of the table at dinner. Bishop Baraga's head and hands were shaking with unwonted agitation, and he was having great difficulty getting the food from his plate to his mouth.

Seeing the Bishop's condition, Captain McKay arose from his seat at the head of the table and ordered Father Chebul to change places with him. Seating himself beside the Bishop, without any word and with great gentleness, he placed one large, firm hand on the Bishop's shaking head while with the other he began lifting the food to the Bishop's mouth. The prelate accepted the kindly service without comment, and ate his whole meal from Captain McKay's hand.

Several ladies at the table were greatly affected by this manifestation of simple kindness. If Father Chebul had done it they would have thought little of it. But the sight of rough, hard-living Captain McKay suddenly become as gentle as a woman was too astonishing. But when, later, they approached him and thanked him for his thoughtfulness, Captain McKay glared at them.

"Thank me, is it? Well, ye needn't! The Bishop is my friend for thirty years. What I did for him he would do for the lowest dirty Injun of the lot of 'em. Once, twenty years ago — " he hesitated, walked over to the rail and looked across the water. Suddenly he turned back to them almost angrily.

"I don't want to talk about it," he snapped, and walked off.

CHAPTER XXVIII

A NATIONAL catastrophe as profound as the War between the States could not but have important effects on even the remotest corners of the country. On Lake Superior it brought marked changes in the social and economic life of the people. Bishop Baraga's responsibilities were multiplied and complicated.

The Marquette iron range had not been long under development at the outbreak of hostilities, and the copper country was just arriving at a period of stabilization, though its most important developments were still in the future. The immediate effect in these mining districts of the beginning of actual conflict was an economic upswing due to the rapid rise in the prices of mining products. When a nation goes to war, copper and iron are prime necessities. Now the market price of copper rose quickly from a level of about fifteen cents a pound to fifty and sixty cents.

But the early enthusiasm was forced to give place at last to a gloom correspondingly deep. The credit system was badly disrupted, with the consequence that money became extremely scarce. Even the best mines were now in a precarious position, a phase of the problem that was immediately dangerous. It was solved to some extent by the mining companies' actually issuing their due bills to serve as local currency — a harmless arrangement which had the merit of success but which later got the company officials into trouble with the government.

Worse than credit difficulties was the problem of the labor supply. Enlistment and finally the draft took many of the ablest men. These were, of course, citizens of the United States. Thus, the great bulk of the laborers left in the district were aliens who were either indifferent to the outcome of the struggle, or if partisan, usually in favor of the South. They were clannish, retained their national languages and remained aloof from American concerns. But they had brought their old-country hatreds to America, with the too frequent result of open, bloody rioting that terrorized whole communities for days. This was particularly true of the Cornish and Irish of that time.

Years afterward one of the leaders of the mining industry remembered that "the winter of 1861-1862 was a most trying one. It was impossible to call on outside help. We faced the prospect of a long and bloody war, unsettled business; and thinking men among us were in great doubt and fear. Bad men were encouraged by the circumstances to lawlessness. As the close of navigation approached, great difficulty was experienced in providing adequate supplies. Indeed, there was a shortage of everything except whiskey, which, under the conditions, should not have been imported at all. It was the cause of untold trouble — fighting, maiming and manslaughter. The number of barrels of whiskey brought in exceeded the number of barrels of flour!"*

Finally — and to Bishop Baraga it brought the deepest concern — a very definite fear of an Indian uprising seized the whole mining area. Wild rumors ran from town to town until the people were not quite responsible in judgment. The northern peninsula (so went the report) was to be stormed from Canada, with great hordes of Indians in the attacking forces. Preparations to resist the attack were actually made and in remote settlements blockhouses of the old American style were

---

*State Senator John H. Forster, in the *Michigan Pioneer and Historical Collections, XVIII*, 375.

He worked as a carpenter to help build the little chapel.

hurriedly built. It was also generally believed that war with Great Britain would come, bringing imminent danger to the people on Lake Superior. The undercurrent of fear ran deep and strong.

In such a crisis, Bishop Baraga was constantly anxious about the uneasy relationship between the Indian and white populations. Any single lawless act by an irresponsible on either side might have dire consequences. Alert and watchful he visited the Indians constantly. He checked on rumors that enemy spies were already among them. In the meantime the annual payments were suspended, making the situation even worse. The Indians suffered from a lack of provisions and their position was made almost unbearable by the suspicions of the white men.

The Bishop's troubles, bad enough in peace, were now much aggravated. Large numbers of the parishioners in the mining towns were foreigners. The diocese lacked priests. Fear of the Indians was real and explosively dangerous. And these problems pressed on an area a thousand miles long, frozen half the year.

There was one brief respite in that trying time. Bishop Baraga went to Sugar Island for two weeks. The October weather was ineffably kind. He lived among the Indians in their lodges and worked with his hands as a carpenter to help them build a little chapel.

That October on Sugar Island, the ancient forest was like a vast pagan temple that seemed to welcome the intrusion of a tiny Christian chapel in its very inner chamber. In the still air the huge maples dropped leaves of scarlet and brown and gold on the bench where the missionary shaped the soft pine boards to construct an altar. The autumn sun lighted and warmed the open space in which the chapel was set. Bishop Baraga was only dimly conscious of the coming and going of the soft-spoken or silent Indians whose guest he was. He had found a kind of sanctuary from all his troubles. The usually shaking hands were quite steady as they fashioned the wood, following the occupation of his Master.

One could almost desire that the story of Frederic Baraga had ended in that sanctuary of peace. The raw and ugly and tumultuous towns were far away. The racial friction, with its outbursts of unchecked passions, was an alien and distant thing. The shock and clash of opposing armies could not penetrate to this quiet place. It was like Lake Superior when he had first come to it. Here the Indians were capable of a natural dignity now possible in few other places. Three generations of them had known and trusted this kind and venerable Blackrobe. He had brought to them no patented ideas of a selfish civilization. Rather, he had searched their hearts for thirty years and built upon the good he found there. Long ago he had planted a seed of Truth in that fertile soil; he had watched and tended it. Now he beheld its growth. He was happy.

CHAPTER XXIX

FOLLOWING that beatific interlude on Sugar Island, the Bishop was plunged back into the turmoil of the times. Old and sick, he was now to know his abysmal hour.

[205]

With the laxity of morals and of law-enforcement that usually accompanies war, the curse of the whiskey traffic with the Indians had increased up and down the diocese. This was igniting a spark close to dynamite, in view of the tense feeling between the Indians and the white inhabitants of the peninsula. Leaders of the northern community, within and without the Church, implored the Bishop to use his influence with the Indians to avert a catastrophe. Even while he promised to do all within his power, he did not neglect to remind these men that it was their duty to see that the law was enforced.

Against the evil times, Bishop Baraga opposed a righteous wrath and a feeble and palsied body. His wrath was for the white debauchers. He had only pity for his Indians. In his extremity, it is true, he sometimes chided those he pitied; but he defended them against prejudiced critics, reserving the hard words for Indian ears alone. In public he would admit that some of them were occasionally "naughty," beyond which mild term he never went in describing their delinquencies.

At L'Anse he heard accounts that shocked and grieved him. There, more than at any other place on Lake Superior, he had stood between his Indians and their own weaknesses. In the mission house were still preserved the signed cards, the pledges given by their elders years before. Now he called a meeting, summoning every Indian. He reviewed all that he had said and done for twenty-five years. He showed them the inevitable consequences of their acts — consequences that would surely destroy them as a people. Using all his force, he pleaded with them.

Then one arose and faced the Bishop.

"It is your own fault," the Indian said. "It is your own fault that we are bad. You spoiled us. You tried to do things for us

"It is your fault that we are bad — you spoiled us."

that could not be done. You spoiled us." And all over the assembly, heads nodded in agreement.

For an awful moment Frederic Baraga was wholly lost. An engulfing wave of despair swept him from his feet and carried him away. It set him down in darkness alone. There all the forces of evil that he had fought for a lifetime hedged him about. For that moment he was defenseless, there on the very soil where he had planted his mission, within the very church that he had built with his own hands.

Those quick pictures that are the essense of a lifetime, that click themselves off in a flash of time, as when one is drowning, came now before his mind. He saw rank and wealth renounced; life itself offered to his mission; tens of thousands of weary, futile miles; all the good years of his manhood cast upon the silent wastes of a cold and hostile country; the heavy hand of age laid upon him until he trembled beneath it. Dear God, are these my rewards?

Now only his heroic humility saved him. If he had been prideful, he might have been truly lost. But he saw clearly, for he saw with the lowliness untainted by self-love, of the great of soul. The record of his mission was almost written, the book was soon to be closed. It would be judged neither by himself nor by any of those whom he had sought to serve.

His face wet with tears, he raised his hand and said in dismissal, "The Lord be with you always."

All that long afternoon and far into the night he talked, face to face, with each of them alone. Most penitent of all was his accuser. He stilled their weeping, brought light into their dark sorrow, set their vision once again upon the Figure on the Cross. To each contrite heart he gave words of wisdom and encouragement.

"My dearly beloved child," he said time and again, "go and sin no more."

The rounds of the diocese were becoming a little too much for the Bishop. He considered: With the expansion of missions westward along Lake Superior, it is probable that those on the lower lakes can soon be more easily administered by the Detroit see. Then we would move, for Sault Ste. Marie would no longer be central. Where might the see be moved? Westward, of course. Father Jacker thought the new and growing city of Hancock on the Portage waterway, in the heart of the now stabilized copper district, would be best. But there was also the promising city of Marquette. Rome must make the decision, and the Bishop thought that the name Marquette would be the determining factor.

The official word from the Vatican was both a permission and an order. The episcopal residence was to be moved to Marquette. The name of the diocese was to remain "Sault Ste. Marie and Marquette."

"Well, I shall use the title Bishop of Upper Michigan except in writing to Rome," the Bishop told Father Jacker with a wry smile. Father Jacker was often with him now, relieving him of such duties as he could. "Never mind about your great city of Hancock," the Bishop went on in mild merriment, to console the disappointed priest. "The librarians and historians at Rome saw nothing in the name Hancock when it was placed beside the name Marquette. You should have got a better name for your city!"

Marquette was already the unofficial capital of the northern peninsula of Michigan, a distinction that it has always retained. From the beginning it managed to avoid much of the raw, ugly appearance of the other new towns on Lake Superior. The iron mines that brought it into existence were a dozen miles away in the interior, so it escaped the drab, utilitarian aspect of the mining location. The little city looked out upon an expansive and beautiful harbor, and behind it picturesque hills rose to shelter it.

To Marquette Bishop Baraga moved in 1866, to establish the seat of his diocese, and to end his mission.

For the end was approaching. His fumbling old hands could scarcely hold a pen to sign his papers. But he would not permit himself to think of the new see as a retreat where he might have the peace and quiet that life owed him. Once settled there, he set forth on a trip that kept him away most of the summer. Nor was his situation as to residence and cathedral very much improved, for he lived in a barren house without comforts and his cathedral, at the beginning, was a parish church.

Conditions in general were better, however. The war was ended and the Union had been saved. The alarms of the people were allayed. The rampage that had been the mining rush finally died down. Men contemplated peace, built homes where they expected to live and die in the midst of families reared in virtue. The speculator and the scamp were lured to other fields. Able priests served all the parishes now. The Bishop's trials had abated at last.

That autumn the Second Plenary Council of the Church in the United States was to meet in Baltimore.

Bishop Baraga thought about Baltimore. He had spent almost his first days in America there. He could recall a multitude of small circumstances that had made that early brief sojourn a happy introduction to the New World. He thought of his fiery visions as he had talked with the Archbishop of Baltimore, youth and maturity facing each other in an interchange of wise counsel and impatient zeal.

Well, he had come to America to be an Indian missionary, and please God he would end his days as one. Perhaps his presence at the Council would be a living reminder of the needs of the Indian missions. Perhaps another Bishop could not be expected to think of the Indian missions in just the way he thought about them. Yes, his going to Baltimore would be part and parcel of his mission itself, perhaps the final act of it. Could he find the strength for the long journey? A boat would take him comfortably to Chicago whence he could continue by railroad. He would try; it was his plain duty to try.

Bishop Baraga kept his eyelids closed and waited and tried to remember. He heard low voices. They could not be far from this bed that felt so clean and soft against his tired old body. Perhaps it would be better never to open his eyes at all but just to wait. . . . Something has happened, he thought. Why were these voices murmuring and whispering? But of course, he was in Baltimore! Or was he? He opened his eyes quickly.

He felt the fingers on his wrist and he turned his head a little on the pillow to see. This is a doctor, he thought. This is a physician sitting beside the bed talking to me. I must listen. I must listen carefully to what he is saying. Or is it really of any importance? But he made a great effort to concentrate his attention.

"You are very much better, Bishop Baraga," he heard the doctor say in competent and kindly tones.

[211]

"Yes? What is it? What has happened?" He wondered at the effort it cost him to use his voice.

The doctor's fingers were still on his pulse.

"Do not talk," he returned quietly. "It is not necessary, and I want you to remain perfectly quiet for a time."

There was a long pause and the doctor seemed to be considering; his fingers never moved from the Bishop's wrist.

"Well, I shall tell you what it is — what has happened," he said finally. "You have had a stroke of apoplexy. Unfortunately, you were at the head of the staircase at the moment, about to descend. It was at the Archbishop's residence. There were others with you but it was impossible to save you from the fall. You fell the length of the staircase."

"This appears to be a hospital," the Bishop said.

The fingers tightened a little.

"Yes," the doctor went on. "Would it surprise you, Bishop Baraga, if I told you that your pectoral cross saved your life? Well, that is true. It saved your life by wounding you. When you fell, the sharp corner of the cross inflicted a wound in your chest which bled profusely. The bleeding saved your life. Otherwise a clot would have formed somewhere to interfere with the action of the heart. And that organ, Bishop, in your case can stand little interference. The wound itself is only superficial and will not trouble you. How old are you, Bishop Baraga?"

The Bishop reckoned. "Almost seventy."

"Seventy — man's allotted time," said the doctor. "The Archbishop has made plans for you to stay here so that you may be easy and comfortable. There is good indication that you are going to be up and around in a few days. But I warn you, no matter how well you may feel in the future, there must be no more of these hardships your friends have been telling me about. Actually, it is not I who give the warning, it is your own heart."

"I am very grateful, doctor, but I have work to do. I am old, and little matters except for my people to —"

The doctor interrupted him. "You must not return to that cold, rough country. No, I don't want you to talk now. But it will be advisable for you to think these things over while you rest here for the next few days."

A more genial climate where life is not so hard — that was the tenor of all the talk he heard while he waited in the hospital at Baltimore.

They did not know — they did not understand. It was difficult for him to talk, it hurt his chest when he tried. How could he describe the dreamworld that October made of Sugar Island while he fashioned a chapel altar? How could he tell them of the clean, cold peace of the winter forest? How could he ever manage to explain that life there was not really hard for him, that it was hard only for his Indians? These friends were exceedingly kind but they did not understand.

He grew restless; he was homesick. The season was advancing; he must not wait too long or navigation would be closed on the lake. Then one day he said to Father Bourion, who had accompanied him to the Council as his theologian, "Now we return home."

Bishop Baraga returned to Lake Superior. He returned literally in the arms of Father Bourion, gasping and panting for each painful breath. On almost the last boat up the lakes that winter, he made a stormy voyage to Marquette.

[213]

CHAPTER XXX

IN THE spring of 1867 the Bishop dictated a letter to a friend: "My health is no better. I can scarcely speak or move. The wound in my chest does not heal. Occasionally I have felt strong enough to take a few steps within the confines of my room."

His household consisted of Father Jacker and Casper, a man-servant. There was little attention he needed. The slight body of the young, lithe Father Baraga had now become the withered body of a tired old man. Casper lifted him as easily as a child. His strength was exhausted. Even when his priests visited him, though he was pleased to see them, he did not encourage them to stay long.

When Father Terhorst, from Assinins, was ready to return thither, he entered the Bishop's room to say farewell.

"You say nothing of your need for money," Bishop Baraga observed. "Take what you find in the box on the table."

The priest found twenty dollars in the box.

"But I cannot take it," he remonstrated. "It is all the money you have."

"You must take it. It is true that it is all I have, but no matter: I came penniless to Lake Superior and I go from it penniless. You will take the money."

Father Jacker said no. But the man persisted.

"The Bishop will be displeased," Father Jacker declared.

"How can I go back without it and tell my sister?" the man implored. "The doctors say she will never walk again. One of the Bishop's stockings is a small thing to you but it might save her life. She is praying for it, Father!"

"This is ridiculous!" exclaimed Father Jacker.

"Well, I'm not so sure," his caller answered. "Old Jean Lassard's foot was so bad that the doctor was going to cut it off. He got up and hobbled on one of Bishop Baraga's old broken snowshoes that an Indian had given him, and his foot healed up. Now Old Jean's as good as new. My sister heard of it. She thinks if she can just wear one of the Bishop's stockings her leg will be cured. It's little enough to try, Father — the doctor says she'll never walk again."

"Tell her to pray."

"But, Father, she is — "

"I tell you finally, no!" Father Jacker exploded.

A feeble voice called from the Bishop's bedroom.

The priest went in while the visitor waited.

"Give the poor anything I have that they need," Bishop Baraga whispered as Father Jacker leaned over him to listen. "I have no further use for anything."

"But you do not understand," the priest began to explain. "The stocking — "

"The stockings will keep some poor person warm. Give them willingly." And the Bishop closed his eyes.

Father Jacker hesitated. It was plain that the Bishop had not understood the use to which the stocking was to be put. But he feared to arouse the sick old man. Out of a chest he took a pair of long woolen stockings and placed them in the visitor's hands.

Watching the man's hurried departure, he began to wonder. Is it possible, he mused, that a Baraga tradition has begun? Is there already in the minds of these people the faith that one

[215]

whose legs have carried him far and wide on long, dangerous missions, can work miracles on diseased limbs? Father Jacker stood at the foot of the Bishop's bed and looked long and thoughtfully upon the frail sleeping figure there.

Wrapped in greatcoats of expensive material, three men were approaching the Bishop's residence. Now and then they stopped in the snow and talked.

"It's not going to be easy to do," Mr. Ely protested. "Here we are, three men outside his Church, going to persuade him to accept our charity. He may resent it!"

"That is true," Peter White agreed. "But it's on my conscience. I am too much indebted — as is every living soul tonight on this northern peninsula — to neglect my plain duty any longer."

"The debt is large," said Philo Everett. "Money can be easily given. But I have a feeling that the debt to Bishop Baraga is beyond payment by coin token. How do you pay a saint with money?"

"Well, I shall not put up with my conscience any longer," Mr. White told them. "That house is as cold and bare as a barn. It hasn't proper furnishings for a Bishop. He deserves better after all these years of hardship and self-denial."

"His own people have tried to do it, and he has refused. We've all heard of their repeated attempts to make him more comfortable. He will not have it!"

"Nevertheless, I am going to try," declared Peter White.

The Bishop received them — it was one of his brief better times when he could sit up in his bed. Their eyes roved over the room. The poor bed, the plain chest, the deal table — the

The mission of Frederic Baraga was complete.

barrenness of his quarters shocked them. Tactfully they approached the object of their visit, retreated, approached again.

"You should have a better bed, Bishop Baraga." It was Peter White who finally ventured the words. "Please allow us the pleasure of providing one. It is a small service that would please us greatly."

"Oh no, my friends! I am as comfortable as need be," the Bishop assured them.

"But we all feel a deep obligation upon us, Bishop. All these years that you have been serving others, bringing quiet and peace and morality to our community, you have become poorer and poorer; while, God forgive us, I myself and these friends and many others of us have been getting richer and richer. Our consciences are stricken."

"It need not be so," the Bishop told them. "I am rich too. For I have acquired what I coveted: I have gained many souls to God. Yes, my friends, I too have grown rich."

It was the feast of the Holy Name of Jesus, which in that year, 1868, fell on the nineteenth day of January. Voices the world over were united in winged supplication, in adoring praise:

Christ, have mercy on us. . . . Deliver us from evil. . . . May Thy blessing sanctify our sacrifice. . . . All the nations Thou hast made shall come and adore before Thee.

Upon the shrunken breast of the Bishop the pectoral cross lifted and fell over the unhealed wound. Now it was a weight upon the feeble breathing. Outside, the winter wind keened about the house — an icy, violent blast from the frozen wastes of Lake Superior. . . .

After a while Father Jacker, his priestly duty done, took the candle from the shaking hand of the manservant.

The mission of Frederic Baraga was complete.

Cum permissu superiorum.

ACKNOWLEDGMENTS

The author is especially indebted for assistance and counsel to the following:

Monsignor Antoine I. Rezek, Houghton, Michigan, for many personal favors which facilitated the writing of this book.

Monsignor Joseph L. Zryd, Chancellor of the Diocese of Marquette, Marquette, Michigan; and Father Ethelbert Harrington, O. F. M., Calumet, Michigan, pastor of the historic Church of the Most Holy Redeemer at Eagle Harbor, Michigan, both of whom gave invaluable encouragement and aid.

Reverend Doctor Hugo Bren, O. F. M., S. T. D., St. Mary's Seminary, Slovene Franciscan Fathers, Lemont, Illinois, who made available to the author materials from European sources collected over many years; and Mr. Joseph Gregorich, Chicago, Illinois, an associate of Doctor Bren in Baraga study, who has been very kind.

Mr. Joseph M. Donnelly, Houghton, Michigan, whose sustained interest and personal assistance have been in the measure of his friendship.

Mrs. Carroll Paul, Marquette, Michigan, who furnished valuable information and an original and revealing letter written by Father Baraga at Arbre Croche in 1833; and Miss Phyliss S. Rankin, Librarian of the Peter White Public Library, Marquette, Michigan, who granted access to old documents and photographs.

Mr. Earl Holman, Antigo, Wisconsin; and Father C. Luke Leiterman, Little Chute, Wisconsin, both of whom gave encouragement and aid.

Miss Catharine M. Breitenbach, Ontonagon, Michigan, who has rendered many kind personal services.

[221]

BIBLIOGRAPHY

1. Primary Source Material

The outstanding original document is the holograph Journal (or Diary) of Bishop Baraga in the Library of the Diocese of Marquette, Marquette, Michigan.

Of almost equal importance are the many holograph letters written by Frederic Baraga as priest and bishop. A large proportion of these were composed in French or German, the latter being chiefly addressed to the Leopoldine Society at Vienna, Austria. Copies of most of these were made by Doctor Bren. A considerable number of holograph letters, in both French and English, are in the hands of private collectors.

While these original documents are not generally available in any public sense, the serious student may have access to them, as the author has had.

2. Published Records of Primary Value

Verwyst, P. Chrysostomus, O. F. M., *Life and Labors of Rt. Rev. Frederic Baraga,* Milwaukee, Wisconsin, 1900. Father Verwyst, himself an Indian missionary priest in the Lake Superior country, quotes many of the Baraga Journal entries verbatim. The book is closest to the scene of the great Bishop's labors, its author had the advantage of knowing personally some of Bishop Baraga's contemporaries, among them Father Edward Jacker.

Rezek, Reverend Antoine Ivan, *History of the Diocese of Sault Ste. Marie and Marquette,* 2 volumes, Chicago, 1907. This work is singularly complete in detail. Monsignor Rezek quotes from the Baraga Journal and letters even more fully than does Father Verwyst, and like him, enjoyed the advantage of personal acquaintance with contemporaries of Bishop Baraga. The work is carefully annotated and altogether scholarly.

Gregorich, Joseph, *The Apostle of the Chippewas,* Lemont, Illinois, 1932. This is a brief popular account of the life and works of Frederic Baraga, carefully written by a notably sincere author who was associated with the work of Doctor Bren. Little is quoted, however, from original sources.

3. Published Works of Close Supplementary Value

Michigan Pioneer and Historical Collections, 1874-1915, Lansing, Michigan. These volumes are collections of articles by hundreds of writers, usually papers read at annual meetings of the Michigan Historical Society, and published by that organization up to 1915. The series is available in most good public libraries, and index volumes will guide the interested reader to pertinent articles, all of which cannot be listed here. Few deal solely with the Baraga story, one of these being by Father Verwyst; but there are numerous articles that touch on the subject, giving good background material, especially (among others) those by Peter White and John H. Forster.

Michigan History Magazine, published by the Michigan Historical Commission, Lansing, Michigan, 1922 to the present, Dr. George N. Fuller, editor; issued quarterly, bound in one volume annually. Numerous articles of supplementary value may be found by reference to the index volume. Cited are three articles by this author: "The Copper Rush of the 50's," XIX, 371; "Captain John G. Parker on Lake Superior, 1846-1870" (which contains Parker's account of a journey with Bishop Baraga), XXIII, 250; and "The Supreme Court Writes Some History" (which has a reference to Frederic Baraga), XXVIII, 466.

4. Published Works of General Supplementary Value

Lanman, Charles, *A Summer in the Wilderness,* New York, 1847.

St. John, John R., *A True Description of the Lake Superior Country,* New York, 1847.

Williams, Ralph D., *The Honorable Peter White,* Cleveland, 1907.

Osborn, Chase S., and Stellanova, *Schoolcraft-Longfellow-Hiawatha,* Lancaster, Pa., 1942.